# Reading
# for Learning
# in the Sciences

The Schools Council Project Reading for Learning in the Secondary School was based at Nottingham University from 1978–1982.

*Project Directors*: Eric Lunzer and Keith Gardner
*Project Officers*: Florence Davies, Terry Greene
*Evaluator*: Roy Fawcett
*Consultants*: Bob Moy, Margaret Berry

# SCHOOLS COUNCIL

# Reading for Learning in the Sciences

## Florence Davies

## Terry Greene

Oliver & Boyd

The cover extract from *Human Biology and Hygiene* by E. J. Ewington and D. F. Moore is reproduced by permission of Routledge & Kegan Paul Ltd

**Oliver & Boyd**
Robert Stevenson House
1–3 Baxter's Place
Leith Walk
Edinburgh EH1 3BB

*A Division of Longman Group Ltd*

© Schools Council Publications 1984
First published 1984

ISBN 0 05 003768 4

Set in Linotron Times Roman 10 on 13 pt

Printed in Hong Kong by
Wilture Printing Co. Ltd.

# Foreword

*Reading for Learning in the Sciences* is one of three volumes arising out of the work of a project carried out at Nottingham University on behalf of the Schools Council during the period 1978–1982. As the title implies, it is addressed to teachers of science and embodies the main principles and methods elaborated by the project, especially adapted for that audience with the collaboration of many scientists engaged in education. Of the two remaining publications, *Learning from the Written Word* is a more general and comprehensive guide to teachers, covering applications throughout the curriculum. This too contains a very large contribution from the writers of the present volume, who were the principal officers employed in the work of the project. The third volume, *Read, Talk, Learn*, will appear in 1985 and contains a full account of the project against the practical and theoretical background in which it was mounted, together with an evaluation of its results and their implications.

In the course of a previous project it had transpired that teachers in British secondary schools had comparatively little faith in the potential of reading as a useful aid to effective learning across the secondary school curriculum. They prefer to rely on a range of techniques, some of which are indeed extremely valuable or even indispensable, but one within which the method of oral exposition combined with question and answer plays an altogether excessive role.

Now there is good evidence both from our own work and from that of other researchers that, left to their own devices, most youngsters are by no means adept at informing themselves through studying text books and works of reference or, for that matter, the handouts offered to them by teachers. Nor is the failure attributable to the deficiencies of the material they are offered, even though much of this is indeed far from perfect. The principal cause of failure is that the first step in learning is understanding, and understanding is a matter of comparing what you read (or what you hear) with what you already know and with what you have just read (or heard). This is what younger readers fail to do. Instead they seem to imagine that, so long as what they read is vaguely sensible and relevant, it will somehow be absorbed – or if not, then that is because they are too dim and there is nothing they can do about it.

Such reading may be called 'receptive'. Receptive reading goes beyond what some educators have called 'barking at print'; it is concerned with 'local sense': the sense that inheres in the clause or the sentence. But reading for learning, especially in the sciences, cannot rest content with such local sense. The reader who would learn must go on to test for overall sense: does this that I have read agree with what was said just before? Does it go beyond what I already know? Does it conflict with what I thought I knew? How must I revise my thinking? That style of reading involves frequent pauses for making these 'coherence checks'; it involves deliberate anticipation, sometimes backtracking. Some have called it interrogating the text. We call it simply 'reflective reading'.

Left to their own devices, most pupils in our secondary schools would learn less well by reading than (even!) by listening. But need they be left? The 'Reading for Learning' project was designed specifically to lead them away from exclusive reliance on receptive reading towards an appreciation of the need for reflective reading, together with an understanding of how to go about it. Previous experience had convinced us that, given the right conditions, reading can be a road to learning, and therefore reading can also be effective and motivating, even exciting.

One of the keys to success was to provide a range of problem-tasks which demand a close and thoughtful study of text for their solution. Informally we called these DARTs: directed activities related to text. The second essential was to devise the lessons in such a way that pupils would be working together in groups. Properly conducted – and a good deal does depend on organisation and on the tasks provided for the group – such work can be purposive, instructive, collaborative, motivating, even exhilarating.

But that is not the whole story. One of the essential features of the work of the 'Reading for Learning' project was an insistence that reading as a technique must be part and parcel of the curriculum and its implementation. Therefore the work was done in collaboration with teachers of all subjects and not just English. *Reading for Learning in the Sciences* is not a set of exercises designed to teach a particular kind of reading. It is a guide to teachers of science which will equip them to devise their own lessons whenever they choose, using extracts from texts that they have selected in accordance with week-to-week (or month-to-month) curricular needs. Such a book would not have been possible without the collaboration of a great many people – teachers, advisers and administrators, all engaged directly or indirectly in the teaching of science and all of whom were willing to devote many hours to collaborating with Florence Davies and Terry Greene to make it possible.

Nevertheless, the principle recognition must go to the authors themselves, both for their own work and for their success in winning the support of others. That support would not have been won were it not that the ideas embodied in the work of the project were in part new and exciting. Particularly important here is the notion of text type or *frame*, which is central to this book. The frames which are so well described and illustrated in Chapters 4 and 5 are like moulds into which the things that one writes about in the sciences tend to fall (as indeed they do in other subjects too), as if of their own accord.

Of course these structures are not spontaneous: they derive from the coherent structure of knowledge in the writers themselves, together with a need to communicate it in such a way that it can be followed, understood, and lead to a similar structure in the mind of the pupil. In science education, the frames fall into three categories: those that describe observations and classify them, those that are used in discussing the theoretical interpretation of such observations, and those that are concerned with what the budding scientist must do to set up the conditions under which observations can be made. Because these things are fairly well defined in the minds of text book writers, they can also be traced in what they write. The techniques for studying texts described in the present volume are specifically designed to bring out the structure of frames. Because the frames themselves have relevance in scientific thinking, work along these lines has been seen as important by science educators.

For some years now, ideas such as this have been nearing the surface of thinking about what makes for coherence in text. Here it has broken through. What distinguishes the text type or generic frame approach from much other work on text analysis is that the latter is nearly always limited to a study of logical or linguistic relations among the sentences and clauses in the passage. By contrast, frames are concerned with the relations between the ideas and the things conveyed by these clauses. It is no accident that such an approach is more relevant to the subject teacher. Florence Davies and Terry Greene did not set out to produce a new way of analysing text. What they sought was a way of using the analytic study of text in a way that would be helpful to the teacher. I believe they have found such a method. At the very least, *Reading for Learning in the Sciences* should be an important stimulus for teachers who are keen on getting children to think for themselves by whatever means are to hand.

Eric Lunzer

# Contents

# Acknowledgements

We wish to thank all who have contributed to this book: the science teachers, advisers, HMIs and colleagues who have developed or tested the reading activities, analysed texts in workshops, raised the issues about the place of reading in science, or contributed to the theoretical underpinning of the book.

In particular we acknowledge a debt to those whose ideas or work are described in this book, namely:

Malcolm Baker, Head of Science, Chellaston School, Derbyshire
Brenda Barratt and colleagues, Castle Donington Community College, Leicestershire
Roger Beswick, Head of English, Priory School, Barnsley
Dr R. Buckley and Dr J. Oliver, Frank Wheldon School, Nottingham
Margaret Clarke, Biology Department, Newfield School, Sheffield
Tony Dimond, Head of Science, Anthony Gell School, Derbyshire
John Heaney, Regional Project Leader (Midlands), Secondary Science Curriculum Review
Dr John Holden, Physics Department, St Ivo School, St Ives, Huntingdon
Dr John Houlding, Chemistry Department, Ecclesbourne School, Derbyshire
David Johnson and Chris Sunley, Stowmarket Upper School, Suffolk
Derek May, Biology Department, High Green School, Sheffield
Mike Poulson, Head of Science, City School, Sheffield
The Science Department, Priory School, Barnsley
Bob Seberry and Alan Swaby, St Thomas More School, Derbyshire
Jim Shimwell, Head of Science, Kirk Hallam School, Derbyshire
and the pupils, whose response has been our major source of encouragement.

We regret that in order to maintain a balance of examples we could not draw upon the work of the many science teachers who have tested or developed materials in their schools. We acknowledge the substantial contribution made by colleagues from:

**Derbyshire**
Anthony Gell School
Belper Upper School
Bemrose School
Chellaston School
Chesterfield School
Clowne School
Ecclesbourne School
Henry Cavendish School
Ilkeston School
Kirk Hallam School
Littleover School
Mortimer Wilson School
Pingle School
St Ralph Sherwin School
St Thomas More School

**Leicestershire**
Castle Donington Community College

**Nottinghamshire**
Frank Wheldon School
Toot Hill School

**Huntingdon**
St Ivo School

**ILEA**
Deptford Green
Dunraven
Forest Hill
Haberdashers' Aske's (Hatcham) Girls
Lewisham

**Sheffield**
City School
High Green School
Newfield School
Norfolk School

**Suffolk**
College Heath Middle School
Elmtree Middle School
Great Cornard Middle School
King Edward VI Upper School
Nacton Heath High School
Pakefield Middle School
St Benedict's RC Upper School
St James CE Middle School
Samuel Ward Upper School
Stoke High School
Stowmarket Middle School
Stowmarket High School
Stowupland High School

We thank HMIs and the advisers in the LEAs who have not only enabled us to work with their schools but who have also provided support for the teachers:
Jack Taylor and Len Jones in Barnsley
Dennis Brook and Reg Hardwick in Derbyshire

John Pearce, Don Cameron and Tom Lyons in Huntingdon
Anne Thomas, Tony Locke and Jeff Kirkham in Leicestershire
Bob Moy, Bob Stammers, Mike Raleigh and Michael Simons in I.L.E.A.
Derek Cronshaw, Jack Ouseby and Jim McLaren in Nottinghamshire
Dave Allen and Brian Harris in Sheffield
Helen Arnold, Giles Job and Les Smith in Suffolk
For the data from the 'Effective Use of Reading' project we are indebted to our directors, Eric Lunzer and Keith Gardner, and to Colin Harrison, Terry and Liz Dolan, and Phil Clarke.

For providing support and guidance in text analysis we wish to thank Eric Lunzer and Nora Byron; and Margaret Berry from the English Faculty at Nottingham University.

Amongst the science colleagues at Nottingham who have monitored our interpretation of science, but who cannot be held responsible for our misinterpretations, are: Richard Hull, Margaret Sands, David Shipstone, Maurice Spenceley and Glyn Yeoman; at Homerton College, Maurice Hornsey and Bob Seberry; and in Suffolk, John Horsfield.

Finally, our greatest debt is to Kay Lunzer and Paula Hill who did a great deal more than type many drafts.


We wish to thank those concerned for permission to reproduce copyright material from the following books:

B. S. Beckett *An Introduction to Biology* © Oxford University Press 1976, pp 94–97, 107–114, 114–124. Reprinted by permission of Oxford University Press

L. J. Campbell and R. J. Carlton (eds.) *Foundation Science*, Routledge Kegan Paul Ltd, 1973, pp 88–90

L. Davies, M. J. Denial, A. W. Locke and M. E. Reay *Investigating Chemistry*, Heinemann Educational Books Ltd, 1976, pp 155–156

T. Duncan *Exploring Physics* Book 2, John Murray, 1970, chapter 2

E. J. Ewington and D. F. Moore *Human Biology and Hygiene*, Routledge & Kegan Paul Ltd, 1971, pp 169, 182–183, 240

D. G. McKean *Introduction to Biology*, John Murray, 1973, pp 22, 96. Reprinted by permission of the author

A. J. Mee, P. Boyd and D. Ritchie *Science for the Seventies*, Heinemann Educational Books Ltd, 1973, pp 42, 97, 107

G. Monger and M. E. Tilstone (eds) *Nuffield Biology 'O' Level Text 1: Introducing Living Things*, Longman, 1974, © Nuffield-Chelsea Curriculum Trust, pp 166–169

C. V. Platts *The Structure of Substances* (Nuffield Background Books) Longman, 1968 © Nuffield Foundation 1968, p 55

C. Ronan *A Book of Science*, © Oxford University Press 1970. Reprinted by permission of Oxford University Press

D. Tinbergen and P. Thorburn *Wreake Valley Project: Integrated Science* Book 1, Unit 5, Edward Arnold, p 25

C. Windridge *General Science* Book 1, Schofield & Sims, 1976, p 42


While every effort has been made to trace copyright owners, apologies are made for any errors or omissions in the above list.

*Note on copyright*
Our objective is to further more extensive use of text books. One of the means towards this end is the marking by pupils of extracts copied from texts used in the classroom. Copyright clearance for the use of texts in this way is always required, as it is for any other form of copying.

Standard pro-formas for obtaining copyright permission are provided by many Education Authorities – or they may have special copyright licensing arrangements and a laid down procedure which should, of course, be followed.

If this is not the case, permission for copying should be sought from the publishers concerned. (See Appendix, page 144 for the details publishers usually require.) Our experience is that publishers are quick to respond to requests for permission to reproduce copyright material and are most often positive in their response.

# Reader's Guide

This book is about three broad issues:

the *place of reading in science education*;
the *range of reading/study activities* which can be used to direct student learning from texts in science;
and the *nature of the texts used in science*.

The book introduces a methodology for reading and learning in science and a methodology for analysing texts. The methodology is the outcome of collaboration between team members of the Schools Council project 'Reading for Learning in the Secondary School', and the science teachers and educators who participated in the project. It also represents the practical application of theories and constructs currently being developed in psychology and linguistics, particularly in text linguistics.

For readers who wish to be selective in their pursuit of these issues, the following guidelines are intended to provide direction.

*The place of reading in science* is explored in detail in Chapter 1. There is also some reference to this issue in the Introduction and in the Annotated Bibliography.

*The set of reading/study activities* introduced in the book are summarised in list form in Table 4, page 48, in Chapter 3, and it is Chapter 3 which focuses in detail on the activities themselves. *Examples of the use of the activities* with specific texts form the substance of this chapter, but further examples are to be found in the Introduction, Chapter 1 and Chapter 5. *A list of all examples of reading activities* illustrated in the book is given in Table 5 on page 73.

The project's approach *to the analysis of texts* is outlined progressively in Chapters 2 and 4. It is introduced in the Introduction and illustrated in Chapter 1. The potential of the approach for providing a *rationale for designing reading activities* is illustrated in Chapter 5. An important outcome of the approach, a *classification of distinct text types or frames* used in science, is to be found in Table 7, page 81.

The *educational and theoretical contexts* in which the methodology has been, and may further be developed, are outlined in the form of an Annotated Bibliography on pages 133–143. There is also some discussion of the educational issues in the Introduction and Chapter 1.

# Introduction

This book is addressed to teachers of science who are interested in promoting more effective learning from the written word. Although the focus of the book is on reading for learning in the sciences, the principles and methods outlined apply in most respects to reading for learning in all subject areas. A more general discussion will be found in the companion volume *Learning from the Written Word*.

The present volume is concerned with what is involved when pupils are required to comprehend and learn from texts in the sciences. The term 'text' is used here to refer to any stretch of written language which can stand on its own as a unit of learning. So it refers to printed material drawn from any source, for instance text books or teacher-produced notes, and to chunks of print varying in length from a paragraph to several pages.

The book is concerned with the kind of reading that is effective in learning science: and with ways in which teachers can provide support and direction for pupils learning from texts.

The basic premises on which the book is based are these:

*1*. Effective reading is active, involving practical activity and hypothesis testing on the part of pupils.

*2*. In science, as in other subjects, there is a limited set of distinct types of text which pupils need to learn to deal with. The types of text identified here are defined not by linguistic features like vocabulary, grammatical complexity or sentence length, but by the nature of the scientific content or information which they present.

*3*. An understanding of the nature of active reading and of the distinct text types of science will enable teachers to provide support and direction for pupil reading.

In the following pages each of these premises is explored in detail. Nevertheless, at this point a simple example will serve to illustrate what is meant by 'active reading' and 'distinct text types' and to show how teachers can make use of these notions in directing pupil study.

## Active reading

The notion of active reading is illustrated in a transcript of a group of ten- to eleven-year-olds studying a text which describes the structure of the tooth. The text is 'Tooth structure' on page 17.

The short transcript demonstrates all the defining characteristics of active reading. There is:

*1. a clear sense of purpose for the reading*: pupils ask questions about what they do not know, but need to know: the function of the parts of the tooth, where they are located, and so on.

*2. generation and testing of hypotheses*: pupils put forward their ideas about the function and position of the parts of the tooth; these ideas are checked against the text and against the stored knowledge of the individuals in the group.

*3. correction and modification of initial interpretations* – note that this correction applies at the level of word identification as well as at the level of meaning identification – as is shown by the correction of the misreading of the word 'projecting';

*4. reference to visual and diagrammatic information* in parallel with reference to the text – note that the use of visual information in this discussion is spontaneous.

## Transcript

(*P*     signifies an individual pupil.
*Sev*     signifies a number of pupils talking across each other.
        Individual contributions are marked at beginning and end by ––.)

*P*     What can we say about the crown?
*Sev*   The crown is at the top –– it's above the gum –– it's the part that's showing –– on the top of the gum ––
*P*     We can put what we think we shall be able to remember it by.
*Sev*   The neck –– is embedded in the soft gum –– it doesn't say –– it's just that bit [pointing to diagram] –– can we just say 'embedded'? – it's where the two bits meet ––
*P*     What about the root?
*Sev*   The root is the bottom part which holds it in place – er – holds it in place –– no, no, the fibres hold it ––
*P*     No, what does it say? – there –– [pupil points] "the root is out of sight anchoring the tooth in its bony socket" – anchoring –– so it does hold it in place.
*P*     I would have thought the root is what they do – anchoring it – the tooth down.

*Sev*   Yes, – – "anchoring it" is what they do – – 'where they are' is at the bottom – – doesn't it tell you on the third line down "in its bony socket".

*P*   Does it tell you what the crown does?

*Sev*   – – protects it – –

*P*   Does it say that?

*Sev*   – yes, part protecting above the gum – –
– it doesn't say protecting does it? – –
– – oh, no projecting – –
– – does it tell you what the crown does? – – doesn't actually does it?

*P*   It's the enamel that – protects it – look, that's enamel [pointing to diagram] around the crown – 'cause your crown is enamel, isn't it? – that's what they're made of, isn't it?

*Sev*   That's what they're made of – – it doesn't tell you what they do. – –
But we know that it protects it, doesn't it? – – What? – –
– – all that does [pointing to diagram] – –
– – it's used for biting and gnawing though, isn't it? – –

The notion of active reading may also be illustrated by asking you, the reader, to practise it. In effect, you have already been invited to practise active reading by being given certain targets to search for in the 'text' of the transcript. Your reading would be more active, and accurate, if, in addition to searching for the targets – pupil questions, pupil hypotheses and checks and modifications of the hypotheses – you were also to underline and label these in the text. This is what the pupils in this lesson were doing. They were searching for and marking information about the parts of the tooth, their function, their properties and their location. They then used this information to construct a table summarising this information.

**Giving pupils specific targets to search for in a text is one way of encouraging active reading. The effectiveness of the search is furthered by collaboration with other pupils.**

This provides pupils with the opportunity to make their hypotheses overt, to have them checked, and to modify them. The activity of physically pinpointing information by marking and labelling gives pupils confidence in dealing with text information, and it encourages accuracy. (See information on permission to reproduce copyright material, pages vi and 144.)

## Distinct text types

**The effectiveness of such pupil activities, however, is largely determined by the teacher's knowledge of the text.**

The teacher who planned a lesson round the text appearing below knew that it was one of a distinct text type – one which describes a 'physical structure' of one sort or another. Texts of this type consistently contain information of certain kinds and (almost) no other information. They contain information about the parts of the structure, their attributes or properties, their location and their function.

**There is a limited number of distinct text types in science, each differentiated according to the sort of information represented.**

Knowledge of the different text types enables teachers to decide quite quickly what text targets they will set for pupils, in accordance with particular purposes.

The notion of distinct text types may be illustrated at this point by inviting you, the reader, to study the complete text on which the pupils worked and to categorise the information in it according to the four categories: 'parts', 'properties', 'location' and 'function'. The most effective way of doing this, we suggest, will be by marking a copy of the text and then underlining (in different colours or keys) the parts of the text corresponding to the different categories. You will also find it useful to follow this up by constructing a table summarising this information. An example is shown in Chapter 4, p. 80, in a further examination of this text type.

---

**Tooth structure**

Teeth are derived from the skin rather than from bone, but they do contain a high proportion of non-living material.

A tooth has three regions: the crown is the part projecting above the gum, the neck is embedded in the soft gum and the root is out of sight anchoring the tooth in its bony socket. Inside the tooth is a fairly hard material which contains some living cells; this is the dentine. The dentine cannot withstand wear, so in the crown and neck it is covered with a layer of hard, non-living enamel. The dentine in the root is covered with a substance called cement, which helps to fix the tooth in its socket. Inside the dentine, in the centre of the tooth, is a hollow pulp cavity containing nerves, a small artery and a small vein.

The teeth are not, however, set immovably in their sockets. If this were the case, we should frequently break our teeth when biting on something unexpectedly hard. Instead, they are suspended by fibres, extending from the dentine to the jaw socket. When we bite, these fibres have a cushioning effect, preventing damage.

From E. J. Ewington and O. F. Moore, *Human Biology and Hygiene.*

We hope that with our initial illustration we have demonstrated the way in which the notions of active reading and of text types can enable teachers to provide support and direction for pupils reading for learning in science.

## The approach to reading in science

We hope also that the illustration provides a basis for a re-examination of the place of reading in science and for a reconsideration of traditional approaches to reading in science. The approach to reading presented in this book is not intended to be an adjunct to traditional practice – it represents a radical, but, we believe, an essentially practical alternative to traditional approaches to text study, notemaking, and, especially, notetaking.

The approach has not developed in a vacuum. It is the outcome of the three years of classroom collaboration between the Schools Council 'Reading for Learning' project team and science teachers and educators committed to furthering more effective use of text in schools. It is the classroom-based work which is represented in the main text of the book.

The approach is also informed by current theory and research into reading and comprehension processes, and into the structure of texts, as we show in the Annotated Bibliography.

But the approach is more directly influenced by the Schools Council project which preceded it: 'The Effective Use of Reading', also based at Nottingham University and directed by Eric Lunzer and Keith Gardner.

This project was concerned with reading across the subject areas in secondary schools. Essentially a fact-finding undertaking, it investigated:

> the incidence of reading;
> the quality of reading in different subject areas;
> the nature of the reading process; and
> the different contexts in which reading took place.

It also initiated a number of pilot studies in which the potential of purposeful, directed-reading activities was examined. The findings of the 'Effective Use of Reading' project and a detailed account of the methods of investigation used are presented in the report of the same title published by Heinemann Educational for the Schools Council in 1979.

Amongst the findings which played a part in the decision to extend the project, and which have a direct bearing on this book, are those to do with:

> the incidence of reading in different subject areas;
> the duration of the reading which did take place in classrooms;
> the level of difficulty of the reading materials used in classrooms; and
> the outcome of two pilot studies on directed reading.

In all subject areas (except, for obvious reasons, English), it was apparent that reading was not a major means of learning for pupils.

The incidence of reading compared with other modes of learning, like listening to teacher exposition, was lower than had been predicted. It was, surprisingly, almost as low in science lessons as in maths lessons.

*Table 1*

| Subject | % of time spent in reading extracted from *The Effective Use of Reading* | |
|---|---|---|
| | Year 1 | Year 4 |
| Science | 9% | 10% |
| Maths | 10% | 8% |
| Social Studies | 15% | 16% |

In all subject areas when pupils were actually engaged in reading, the duration of the read was remarkably short; most reading observed in classrooms occurred in short bursts of less than 30 seconds.

The reading materials of science and social studies, assessed according to a number of readability criteria, were found to be most difficult for pupils, with first-year science standing out as particularly difficult.

Included in texts assessed to be very difficult were teacher-produced as well as commercially-produced materials. Marginally the most 'difficult' of all texts were those used for homework.

The general picture which emerged was that of a substantial retreat from print, for which we seek an explanation in Chapter 1.

Against this background some more promising data were also collected. These were the results of two small pilot studies in which teachers experimented with *techniques for directing pupil reading*. In these situations pupil performance seemed to be more effective than it was when reading was undirected. Phil Clarke, a science teacher in Nottinghamshire, found that pupils performed better in practicals, and understood the scientific principles of a topic better, when the experimental work was preceded by a closely-directed reading activity. In another study, teachers explored the potential of a number of directed-reading activities in collaboration with the project team. Subjective evaluation of the activities was positive and it was decided to extend the programme.

The evidence suggested that the conditions under which effective reading occurred could be controlled by teachers. As a consequence, the brief of the 'Reading for Learning' project was to refine and extend the procedures which could be used by teachers to further effective reading in the sciences and humanities.

In fulfilling this brief, the project team and collaborating teachers have been concerned to develop procedures which would involve pupils in active reading; which would direct pupil attention to key information in science texts; and which pupils could build into their own independent study skills.

From the start of the work, however, it was apparent that the design or choice of reading activity could not be made without taking account of the sort of text which was being used. So a further objective was formulated: that of developing a system for describing differences amongst texts.

**The issues of how to read in science and what is read, it was clear, cannot be treated separately. Nor, it was to become apparent, can they be considered in isolation from questions about the place of reading in science.**

It is the teachers who initiated discussion about the place of reading in science; it is the first issue we address.

# 1
# The Place of Reading in Science Education

## Learning in science: a practical base

**If reading has a place in the science curriculum, it is a place which must be justified alongside other modes of learning which are seen to be important.**

Foremost, in the view of the science teachers with whom we have worked comes practical experience and observation. The commitment of teachers to a practical base for science has been emphasised by them throughout the course of the 'Reading for Learning' project's work and is expressed in observations like:

> "There is no substitute for group practicals and demonstration as a means of achieving initial experience and learning."

> "Although it is possible to learn non-practically, such an approach is undesirable and likely to reduce rather than increase children's interest."

> "Our course is practically-based and texts are used infrequently."

Certain basic assumptions underpin this practically-based approach to science: that active participation in scientific activities and procedures is fundamental to the learning of science (see Aims of the Association for Science Education, 1980), and that such active involvement on the part of pupils will develop predictive thinking and increase motivation to learn. The translation of these assumptions into classroom realities owes a substantial debt to curriculum innovation initiated by the ASE, the Nuffield Foundation, and the Schools Council.

That most teachers accept the centrality of practical experience in science education is confirmed in the recent HMI survey of secondary schools (HMSO, *Aspects of Secondary Education*, 1979). Furthermore, science teachers in the majority of schools of all types are apparently effective in implementing practical courses.

We share with our science colleagues the view that practical experience is central to science education. Practical experience provides for pupils the opportunity to:

practise scientific methodology;

generate and test hypotheses;

share and revise interpretations of data; and
solve problems.
It also encourages pupils to take responsibility for their own learning.
**In sum, practical experience encourages active learning.**
It involves pupils in the process of science and gives them a foundation for
the learning of content.
**Nevertheless, this practical base needs to be supplemented by other learning
activities which help pupils to master the content of science.**
The best practice, in the view of the HMIs, involves "Group practical work
... with sensible support from classroom teaching, demonstration, use of
text books, theoretical work and notemaking."

**Allocation of time to different modes of learning in science**

Thus, in the presentation of content, teachers have the option of giving
pupils experience of a number of other modes of learning in addition to
practicals.
Data from 'The Effective Use of Reading' project summarised in Table
2 below show the percentages of time allocated to different activities.

*Table 2*
*Time spent in different activities by first
and fourth year pupils as % of total science time*

| Activity | Year | % of time |
|---|---|---|
| Practicals | 1 | 23 |
| | 4 | 11 |
| Observing | 1 | 7 |
| | 4 | 8 |
| Reading | 1 | 9 |
| | 4 | 10 |
| Writing | 1 | 11 |
| | 4 | 20 |
| Listening | 1 | 26 |
| | 4 | 31 |
| Non-involved | 1 | 8 |
| | 4 | 10 |
| Discussion | 1 | 13 |
| | 4 | 10 |

Note: *1.* Activities observed were not always mutually exclusive.
     *2.* Other activities observed included administration, calculating and de-
liberating. See Chapter 5 of *The Effective Use of Reading*, pp 108–122.

The activities fall into two broad categories: those which provide practical experience, namely practicals and observation, representing 30% of
pupil time in the first year, and 19% in the fourth year; and those activities
which involve the processing of information, namely listening, reading
and writing, occupying, in total, 46% of pupil time in the first year and
61% in the fourth year.

Our concern here, however, is not with the relative amount of time
spent on practicals as opposed to information processing. This is properly
the concern of science teachers who have clear criteria for evaluating the
overall balance between the two modes of learning.

**We are interested in the balance between the different information-
processing activities, specifically between those activities which,
by definition, assign pupils a passive role in learning, like listening,
notetaking and copying, and those which, at least potentially, allow pupils to
take an active role, like reading, note-making and personal writing.**

The data show that, outside practicals, a large proportion of pupil time is
occupied in passive activities. Listening alone accounts for 31% of pupil
time in the fourth year. When the writing category is broken down into
types of writing, as it is in table 5.3 in *The Effective Use of Reading*, the
figures show that in year one 71% of writing activities are passive, involving copying (46%) or answering (25%), and in year four 73% (56%
copying and 17% answering).

In contrast, note-making and personal writing constitute only 29% of the
writing activities in the first year and 27% in the fourth. Amongst all the
activities, reading is allocated only 9% of pupil time in the first year and
10% in the fourth, the total for the two year groups constituting 1% less
time than that spent in the non-involved category.

In the following pages we seek an explanation for the low incidence of
reading and for the extensive reliance on passive modes of learning.

## Reading in science

There is no doubt that science teachers have very clear conceptions of what
reading and its outcomes should be. It should involve an active response to
text and result in selective and structured notemaking. Pupils, however,
rarely fulfil these expectations:

"I don't feel satisfied that the kids actually use the texts."
"Teachers often find that when children are set to read a passage they
get little real understanding from it."
"Lack of pupil competence in notemaking is a cause for concern for
many teachers."

"Occasionally they make notes from a text book. This tends to be straight copying and no real reading of the text takes place."

"The requirement to take notes as they read too often results in unashamed copying or crude paraphrasing."

These observations suggest that pupils are reading passively rather than actively.

### Passive reading

**Passive reading occurs when reading purposes are vague and general rather than specific, and when reading is solitary rather than shared.**

Traditionally, most reading in science has been solitary; it has been undertaken for general as opposed to specific purposes.

Reading for homework, constituting 37% of homework in science for the first year pupils and 45% for fourth year pupils (J. Cole in E. Lunzer and K. Gardner *The Effective Use of Reading* 1979) is almost always solitary. John Heaney (chairman of ASE, 1980–81) observes that in the homework situation "children are asked to handle a difficult technique without immediate teacher support, or even, in most cases, appropriate advice on the purpose of the task."

In both the homework situation and in the classroom, reading purposes are no more specific than "read these pages/chapter for revision or a test" or "make notes from this section". Giving a general instruction like this is analagous to giving pupils a general instruction to do an experiment without any indication of the particular purpose of the experiment, or of how to go about doing it.

### Active reading

**Active reading, in contrast to passive reading, involves reading for specific purposes.**

Pupils are instructed to search a text for specific information about a topic, for instance, descriptions of the parts of a plant. They are shown how to classify this information in appropriate ways, for instance, into descriptions of the features of the parts and their functions. The text is treated as a set of data; it is analysed. The results of the analysis are discussed by pupils working in small groups and/or contributing to a teacher-led discussion.

In the active situation, pupils are alerted by the teacher to the nature of the material they are using, and they are provided with the tools for dealing with it. They are also given the opportunity to practise. In many ways, active reading parallels the methodology of science practicals.

Ideally, this practice takes place in the presence of a coach who knows the materials and tools and who closely monitors pupil practice. In our view it is only the science teacher who is equipped to do this.

**Active reading in science thus requires the involvement of teachers willing to provide support and direction for reading.**

There is little evidence to suggest that this kind of support for active reading is widely available to pupils.

Outside practical lessons it seems that teachers have little confidence in their pupils' capacity for active learning. Furthermore, the managerial skills so successfully used for directing learning in practicals are not being utilised to train pupils in active learning of content from texts.

It is in the context of the practical situation that we introduce our second example of active reading. The text contains instructions for carrying out an experiment. The teacher has provided a good deal of specific direction and support. The pupils in this instance are two nine-year-olds working on an experiment whilst studying electricity.

---

**The text**

Here is another way of finding out about charges. You have four strips of plastic. Two are cellulose acetate (the clear ones), the others are polystyrene (the opaque ones – the ones you cannot see through). Rub one of these strips with a duster and then balance it on the watch glass. Now bring it near a rod of the same kind which you have rubbed with the same duster, and observe what happens as you bring the ends near each other. Do they attract or repel? Each strip has obviously been given the same charge because they were both treated exactly the same way. What do like charges do to each other?

Now repeat the experiment using two strips of the other material. Do they attract or repel one another? Does this agree with what you found in the first part of the experiment?

Now rub a strip of one material and balance it on the watch glass, and bring up to it a strip of the other material which you have also rubbed. What happens this time? Can the charges be alike? If they are not they must be opposite or 'unlike'. What can we say unlike charges do to each other?

From A. J. Mee, P. Boyd and D. Ritchie, *Science for the Seventies*.

---

In addition to the text, pupils were provided with the appropriate equipment and the following list of instructions:

---

**Worksheet**

*1.* First read the complete passage on the sheet to the end.
*2.* Decide together how many experiments are described.
Draw a line across the page between each experiment, and
number the experiments.
*3.* (*a*) For the *first experiment, underline* in pencil the names
           of any *pieces of apparatus* you will need.
     (*b*) Put a *circle* round the words which tell you *what to do.*
     (*c*) *Underline* in *red* any *questions* you see.
*4. Do the first experiment.*
*5.* For the *second* experiment, again underline *the pieces
of apparatus*, circle the words telling you *what to do*,
and underline *questions* in red.
*6. Do the second experiment.* And so on, until you have finished all
the experiments.
*7.* Finally, look again at the *questions* you have underlined.

---

What was the purpose of the instructions?

The first objective was to ensure a very thorough *rehearsal* of the practical activities before actually doing them; this included identifying the separate experiments. The second objective was to provide pupils with a systematic *procedure* for undertaking an experiment: identifying the apparatus required, and the procedures to follow. A third objective was to get pupils to reflect on the purpose of the experiment *before* undertaking it, hence the emphasis on the questions.

Extracts from a transcript of the discussion between pupils as they follow the instructions suggests that these objectives were achieved.

Given below are three short extracts from the transcript of the taped discussions. The numbers on the left hand side, eg 04.00, show the passage of time in half minute intervals; P1 and 2 are the two pupils concerned. The extracts come from the start, middle, and end of the session and show the pupils actively organising materials, method and results through positive guided interaction with the text.

**Transcript**

00.00  1.  Pairs read Worksheet 1

00.50  2. Pairs read text through (Sheet 2)
01.00–03.50  (Start with Instruction 2 from Sheet 1)

    *P1*  Do you think that is one?

04.00  *P2*  That is [points para 1] but that isn't [para 2] because,
         er . . . it . . . you're not doing anything different.
         (Runs finger under and reads
         *Rub one of these strips with a duster and then balance it on the*
         *watch glass.*
         *Now repeat the experiment using two strips of the other material.*)

04.50  *P1*  I think that is [para 2] because it's '*other material*'.

    *P2*  . . . and that is [para 3].
        (Second reference which is read
        *Now rub a strip of one material and balance it on the watch glass –*
        again finger is run under text)

    *P1*  Have you decided how many experiment there are?

    *P2*  There's one there [points para 1] and there [points para 2] – I'm
        not sure about these three passages (paras 3,4,5). I am going to
        read them slowly so I can get them right.

05.00  (*P1* re-reads instructions from Sheet 1, *3.(a),(b),(c)*.)
    *      In 3.(a)  For the first experiment underline in pencil the names
             of any pieces of apparatus you will need.
          (b)  Put a circle round the words which tell you what to do.
          (c)  Underline in red any questions you see.

    *P2*  In pens or in pencils?

    *P1*  *Four strips of plastic* . . . er . . . *a duster . . . a watch glass . . . a*
        *rod* . . . er . . . that's the plastic thing again. . . .

05.00  *P2*  . . . *watch glass . . . duster*

    *P1*  Right, what's next?

    *P2*  Isn't there any more in the whole passage?

06.00  *P1*  It's in the first, 'cause that's the first experiment.

    *P2*  Right, let's have a look for these [words] now.
    *      (re-reads instruction 3. (*b*) from the worksheet
        "Put a circle round the words which tell you what to do.")
        The next lot are this [points para 1].
        In the whole passage?

06.30  *P1*  In the first experiment . . . put a circle round the words which tell
        you what to do.

07.00  *P2*  What've you put, N?

    *P1*  *Rub one of these strips with a duster . . . then balance it on the*
        *watch glass.*
        *. . . now bring it near a rod.*

07.50  *P2*  . . . *which you have rubbed with same duster.*

---

* Indicates direct reference to worksheet (Sheet 1).
  Direct reference to text (Sheet 2) is in italics.

    *P1*  Right, we've done that.
    *P2*  What does it say to do next?
    *P1*  Er (re-reads *3. (c)* from Worksheet 1
  *         "Underline in red any questions you see")
        *. . . Do they attract or repel?*
    *P1 What do like charges do to each other?*

The pupils go on to carry out experiments 1 and 2 according to the instructions. We pick them up again 12 minutes into their work.

12.00 *P1*  Shall we do the next experiment now?
      *P2*  Ｎo, let's just do this again. It's not going.
      *P1*  It is . . .
      *P2*  It is, as it turns, it goes the other way. It just did the same really
            as the other one.
      *P1*  Right, now we've got to do it. *Rub a strip of one material, and*
            *balance it on the watch glass . . . so one material . . . watch*
            *glass . . . other material.*
12.50     [these are underlined]
           Right, now we can start.
      *P2*  What have we got to do, N?
      [N (*P1*) re-reads first sentence, para 3; G carries out experiment,
      *Now rub a strip of one material . . . and balance it on the watch*
      *glass . . . and bring up to it a strip of the other material which you*
      *have also rubbed.*]
13.00 *P2*  Gosh, look at that!
      *P1*  Moving like mad, that . . . going the opposite way.
      *P2*  You could have an aeroplane with it going at that rate.
           Hey, we could solve the energy crisis.
      *P1*  Give me that cloth! Let's do this third one again!
13.30     [rubs strips]
           I'll put it on. It's kind of attracting it.
      *P2*  It seems to dip.
      *P1*  It's making it move. It's repelling it, isn't it?
      *P2*  At one end.
      *P1*  At one end it repels.
14.00     [*P1* re-reads the whole of para 3:
      "*Now rub a strip of one material and balance it on the watch glass,*
      *and bring up to it a strip of the other material which you have also*
      *rubbed. What happens this time? Can the charges be alike? If they*
      *are not they must be opposite or unlike*".]
      [*P1* re-rubs two unlike strips.]

14.30 *P1*  Now see what happens. Wowee, it's attracting it. It's going
round like mad. Is that how they make aeroplane propellers
work? [mutters and re-experiments]
It's doing it again. It's that end that does it.

*P2*  Can I have a go after you, N?

Towards the end of their discussion they decide what it is that they have
discovered.

15.50 *P1*  [Reads *Can the charges be alike?*] Some have got to be, haven't
they?

*P2*  No, they're probably kind of magnetic. That's why they . . .

*P1*  They're different . . . they're repelling. If they do the same thing
it doesn't matter.

*P2*  [still experimenting] What are these doing?
[repeating experiments 1 and 2]

16.00 *P1*  They're repelling. And the others were attracting. Can I have a
go?

*P2*  So, how many charges are they . . .

*P1*  Because one attracts, one repels . . .

*P2*  Yes, because [still experimenting – alternating experiment 1
and experiment 3] one goes like that, and one goes like that.
When we used this one and that one, the clear materials, the
clear ones – they were going like this [demonstrates].

16.50 *P1*  So there must be one thing that attracts them and one which
repels it.

*P2*  And, er . . . it's slanting though, isn't it?

*P1*  Does that kind of direction matter? It's because of the balance.

17.00  *What can we say unlike charges do to each other?*

*P2*  That's a clear one and a thick one. ck one.

*P1*  Well, they attract each other, and the same ones don't.

*P2*  We could write that down.

17.50

In addition to the short-term objective of encouraging more active reading
and practical work, there is a longer-term objective in the sort of work
described above. This is to give pupils a framework for using *instruction-
type texts.*

**Instruction-type texts comprise by far the greatest proportion of reading
material in science lessons in the early years of secondary schooling.**

The basic framework pupils were given in this lesson: Experiment: *apparatus + procedure or steps + interpretation,* is one which they can apply to

other material of the same type, and which they can build on and amplify until it approaches the more complete framework described in Chapters 4 and 5.

The acquisition by pupils of appropriate frameworks for active reading is, as we have shown, critically dependent upon the provision of such frameworks by the teacher. It is also dependent upon the provision of appropriate reading material.

## Resources for reading in science

Further data from *The Effective Use of Reading* summarised in Table 3 show that a number of different sources of written material are used for reading in science, namely: teacher-produced notes, worksheets, blackboard notes, reference books, and pupil-produced notes.

*Table 3*
Types of reading material presented to first and fourth year pupils in science lessons.

| Reading material | Year | Percentage |
|---|---|---|
| Reference | 1 | 7 |
|  | 4 | 2 |
| Library book | 1 | 30 |
| Text book | 4 | 13 |
| Blackboard | 1 | 22 |
|  | 4 | 25 |
| Exercise book | 1 | 14 |
|  | 4 | 43 |
| Others, including teacher-produced worksheet | 1 | 27 |
|  | 4 | 18 |

Nevertheless, teacher-produced texts in the format of blackboard notes or worksheets constitute the major source of written material, accounting for 49% of texts used in year one and 43% in year four. Text books accounted for only 13% of the materials read in year four, with a surprisingly higher incidence of use, 30%, in year one.

# Availability and quality of resources for reading in science

## Availability

**It may be supposed that one reason for a reliance on teacher-produced materials is a lack of financial resources for the purchase of materials.**

As noted in *Aspects of Secondary Education*: "Science is a practical subject and departments have decided that they must, as far as possible, maintain their stocks of apparatus. Doing this often used up most of their financial resources so that little was left over for books" (Chapter 6, para 6). In the view of the HMIs, provision of books is adequate in *only half* of the full range of comprehensive and grammar schools (Chapter 8, para 6).

## Quality of resources: text books

**In addition to a lack of textual resources, teachers' evaluation of text books may also be a factor contributing to a reliance on teacher-produced texts.**

Teachers' judgements about text books vary considerably, reflecting the wide and often idiosyncratic range of criteria used in evaluation.

On one criterion, however, teachers are agreed: most published texts are rated as 'too difficult' or, alternatively, lack coherence and are confusing. Only the quality of diagrams in most modern text books is consistently highly rated. Data on the readability of texts from *The Effective Use of Reading* support the teachers' views. For both first- and fourth-year groups, science and social studies contain the most difficult texts, with first-year science standing out as particularly difficult (*The Effective Use of Reading*, page 85). Furthermore, "Texts set by teachers to read for homework on their own turned out to be more difficult than those used in class." Further evidence of the severe demands on learners made by science text books is provided by Gould (1977). In an analysis of three widely used biology books for the 13–16 age range he found the reading levels of the books to be at the 17–18-year-old level.

It is not surprising, then, that teachers lacking confidence in pupil capacity to handle text independently, and lacking confidence in the texts themselves, feel an obligation to pre-process information for oral presentation to their pupils. It is also to be expected that teacher-produced materials will be a major resource for learning in science.

What might not have been predicted is the substantial use made of pupil's own notes as texts. These constituted 43% of all the material read by the fourth-year pupils, equal to material produced by teachers and outweighing the use of text books in the pre-examination year, when an increase in the use of text books might have been expected.

## Quality of different resources: published texts, teacher-produced texts and pupil-produced texts

**If the quality of text books varies, so too, it must be acknowledged, will the quality of teacher- and pupil-produced texts.**

One of the most obvious differences between a text book and material produced by a teacher or pupil is the form or state of the draft. Text books, by virtue of being published, are in the form of 'final' draft – they have been extensively edited, re-written and re-edited.

By contrast, most pupil notes represent initial drafts. Teacher-produced worksheets, blackboard notes and dictated notes clearly fall at points along the continuum from initial to final draft.

**When evaluating the quality of textual resources, the state of the draft is clearly an important factor.**

Final drafts have of necessity been worked over, checked for accuracy and revised for publication. They may have features which make them difficult for certain audiences to read, but they will be coherent and relatively free of inaccuracies and ambiguities.

By contrast, initial draft texts are likely to contain a high proportion of errors and inaccuracies. They may be more or less accessible to their writers, but they are likely to lack coherence and to be incomplete, as every teacher marking pupil notes is aware.

### Teacher-produced text

Teacher-produced material, like published material, is unlikely to contain inaccuracies, but because it is not the final draft, and rarely subjected to external editorial processes, it is likely to contain ambiguities. Furthermore, there is no guarantee that teacher-produced texts, per se, will present information more effectively than published texts. As the 'Effective Use' survey showed, teacher-produced texts may not even be easier than published texts. The language level of much teacher-produced material was found to be much higher than that of comparable published texts, and the layout very much worse.

**The evidence suggests that the pre-processing of information for pupils in the form of notes and worksheets by teachers does not make the problem of text book difficulty go away.**

Indeed it often results in the provision of textual resources which are less accessible to pupils than published texts. Both text books and teacher-produced materials exhibit features which can potentially create difficulties for pupils if they are reading passively.

But, as we have already illustrated, and show in detail in subsequent chapters, the best of these resources are also coherent and structured in ways which teachers and their pupils can take advantage of.

### Pupil-produced texts

By contrast, the texts produced by pupils are much more variable in structure and coherence, and they are not necessarily the best resources for revision purposes. The reasons for the extensive reliance on pupil notes recorded in *The Effective Use* survey have not been formally articulated. One justification might be that examination pupils are required to rely on notes as a major textual resource. For many pupils, their own notes provide security. Furthermore, the activity of *making notes* is an important means of learning in itself; 'good' notes are a by-product.

But if pupil notes are to be consistently good, and are to serve as an adequate textual resource, their quality needs to be ensured. The notes used for revision and reading need to be more than initial draft. They need to be worked over, and they need ideally to draw upon more than one original source of information.

### Dictated notes

The traditional solution to the problem of imperfect notes is the *dictation of notes* by the teacher. This procedure, still widely practised according to the HMI report *Aspects of Secondary Education*, is designed to ensure, first, that notes are more coherent and error free than those made by pupils, and second, that there is no individual variation in texts, apart from handwriting. On the surface, the dictation of notes provides consistency and security for teachers and pupils. In practice, it serves as a barrier to learning in a number of different ways.

Dictated information has a status or authority which it may or may not deserve. But being presented *orally* to a passive audience, it is not open to scrutiny by pupils, or by the teacher, in the way that *written* text is.

Second, pupils who have notes dictated are restricted to a single source of information rather than several.

Third, the dictation of notes prevents pupils from taking an active part in notemaking. It encourages them to be dependent and fails to provide them with the opportunity to practise the skill of notemaking. It gives them no guidance about how to make adequate notes or about how to identify and use text structure.

Finally, it involves pupils in a mechanical copying task and thus prevents them from learning. Copying notes from oral presentation or from the black-board is laborious and time-consuming. It requires concentrated attention which is focused on the *mechanics of recording* instead of on the *processing of information*. The task of copying precludes attention to content.

**Pupil reading and notemaking in science is unlikely to improve in efficiency or quality as long as information is pre-processed by teachers. A method which is intended to provide support for pupil learning of content in practice works against it.**

## The place of reading in science: an alternative approach

"The first step in any reform," John Heaney argues, "should be a recognition by teachers of the intrinsic importance of reading in science. If we take this first step it has pedagogic implications. We have then to accept a professional obligation to *teach* the necessary techniques and to provide suitable texts. This requires a time allocation in schemes of work and a teaching strategy."

Furthermore, "Reading is not a natural activity and reading of scientific texts is a specialised technique requiring skills additional to those needed for general reading."

We are confident that science teachers who have participated in the development of the approach described in this book endorse this view. There is widespread agreement about the necessity to accept responsibility for pupil use of texts. Teacher direction of reading in science is increasingly regarded as being as important as teacher direction of practicals. Reading in science is distinct in many significant ways from reading in other subject areas and as such needs to be taught by scientists.

**A commitment to furthering reading in science is ideally manifest in a willingness to experiment and evaluate. This has been widely demonstrated by teachers collaborating with the project.**

All have been prepared to arrange for some class time to be made available for text-based lessons, and to try a range of techniques. The proportion of time devoted to reading activities varies from teacher to teacher and also with the teacher's experience of reading for learning activities. Teachers experienced in the directed-reading activities are increasingly allocating more time to text-based lessons with their examination pupils. Across the age-range, a minimum of three text-based lessons per term with a given class is seen to be a practical objective. Teachers who have tried new techniques have been careful to evaluate their relative merits for different purposes.

"Directed-reading activities, especially *sequencing* and deletion (see

Chapter 3 for an explanation of sequencing and deletion), have been useful and effective as a revision tool; the former for reinforcing knowledge of lab procedures and the latter for establishing theory and principles. *Underlining* has been effective and, I feel, more interesting to children in teaching topics which otherwise would be mainly taught by teacher 'lecture', often backed up by films, slides."

"It has been possible to draw out historical and geographical and interdisciplinary connections which would have been difficult to produce otherwise."

**The close link between directed reading and note*making* has also been recognised.**

"Notemaking from text is a different skill (from reading) although closely related and this, if it is to serve a useful purpose, has to be taught in a structured, though not necessarily formal, way. Many directed-reading activities provide an interesting model for this process."

Furthermore, if pupils are to become independent and confident in their reading and notemaking by the time they reach examination classes they need to be trained before they reach the fifth year and need to continue to receive guidance throughout their schooling.

A careful evaluation of the relative effectiveness of alternative resources for learning is also required. The allocation of lesson time to directed reading does mean that less time is available for other activities. A choice has to be made.

**For most teachers it is 'lecture' and notetaking time which is used for directed reading.**

In the light of such costing, directed reading is seen by many teachers to be effective.

"The process is longer than 'lecture' but it is often offset by the time taken (in class and at home) in making decent notes from rough, or in dictating notes and drawing diagrams from the board."

While changes in syllabus can and do come about as an indirect result of changes in practice, this is not a necessary corollary of directed reading in science. No modification to the syllabus is suggested by the project team or by teachers. Without exception, text-based lessons are on topics already planned in the ongoing syllabus. The texts are those already in use in the classroom or are supplementary materials appropriate to the topic.

**The limitations of textual resources have been accepted by teachers and the project team from the start. The effect has been to make us aware of our**

**responsibility to provide support for pupils reliant on resources which are far from ideal, and to make sure that we know our texts.**

"The majority of pupils do not use texts effectively – this is no reason to abandon them. If we cannot change the texts and the children we have to change the approach to using texts."

Pupils need practice and training in reading and comprehension strategies. Pupil practice and training in reading is nevertheless dependent upon teachers' knowledge of their texts.

**All the text-based lessons which have been implemented in the project are preceded by a careful analysis of the text.**

This has been undertaken either by a member of the project team, by the teacher, or by a group of teachers and members of the team. The purpose of the analysis is to find out:

*1.* what is in the text;
*2.* what is not in the text;
*3.* what distinct text type it is;
*4.* what problems are likely to be encountered by pupils,
and to construct a framework for active reading.

This detailed knowledge of the text supplements the teacher's lesson objectives, and his or her knowledge of the pupils. Together they form the basis on which a reading activity is planned.

## Summary

In science, reading for learning is not an alternative to the practical approach through observation and experiment. It is an adjunct. The methods that are described in this book are active and sharply focused. They have much in common with science practicals.

Many teachers would like pupils to learn from text but have hitherto been unsuccessful in finding the time, or the right texts, or the right method. The time can be found not at the expense of practicals but at the expense of things like dictation, oral exposition, and mechanical exercises. No text is ideal, but published texts in science are often far better than might be thought from the widespread reliance on teacher and even pupil notes. The key to success in learning from any text in science is the choice of the right method to get the most out of it. This involves an understanding of the ways in which texts are structured – the subject of the next chapter.

# 2
# The Nature of Reading in Science: the Text and the Task

How are the texts of science to be described; in what ways do they differ from texts in other subject areas; and how does the text influence the reading task?

## Features of text: communication and information structure

We have seen that reader purpose will influence the nature of the task; so, too, will the nature of the text being read. The texts of history, geography, English and science are apparently different. We want to be able to describe the specific features which give rise to differences, and also to similarities, in texts across the subject range.

In order to do so we depart from tradition: our analysis does not start with the surface features of a text, like terminology, sentence length, or readability level, but with the underlying elements of meaning or information[1] on which texts are based. It is our intention to show that it is what these are and how they are organised which largely determine the reading demands of different texts. Science teachers, we believe, are concerned with helping their pupils to get through the language of text to the underlying content. This is why the focus of our analysis is on what we call the *information structure* of the text.

In order to achieve some precision in defining *information structure* we need to differentiate the information structure of a text from the way in which a text is organised as a *communication*.

## Writer intention in organising a text as a communication

The way in which a text is organised as a communication is controlled by the writer. As communicators, writers have different *intentions*: to entertain, or to persuade, or to inform, and so on. In order to achieve one or more of these general intentions, writers take care to organise what they are saying as a communication. They make choices at a number of different levels. They *select, from a set of possible alternatives, the words or phrases*

37

which best serve their purpose; they decide how best to *organise these elements within sentences*; they make decisions about the *best order* in which to present *the different elements of information* in sentences and paragraphs; and they make use of a variety of devices for *linking one part of the communication with another*. The product of such decision making, when it is successful, is a *cohesive*, integrated text which clearly reveals the writers' communicative or pedagogic intentions.

In the case of science texts the writer's intention is usually to inform: to describe, explain, and initiate readers into ways of observing, thinking about, and doing things. Thus the choices made by writers of science texts are choices to do with how best to organise the information accurately and clearly. But the information itself is, for the most part, given. That is to say, a writer has very little choice about the *facts* he or she is presenting, only about how to express them and organise them in written, graphic or numerical form, in a way that will communicate to his or her readers. Thus, in organising the text as a *communication on one level*, a writer draws upon *another level of knowledge – the underlying information*.

When, as teachers, we are concerned with *writing* or with providing support for *pupil writing*, we, too, ensure that pupils have a solid experiential or information base from which to write. But in providing guidance for the writing which arises from this base, our focus, like that of the writer, is on how a text may be organised as a communication.

However, when we are *reading* or providing guidance for *pupil reading*, our concern is not so much with the way a text is organised as a communication (though this will sometimes be the focus of study in English lessons) but with what it is that is being communicated: the underlying, new information.

## Information structure

It is the underlying level of information communicated through text which we want our pupils to reach. Furthermore we want our pupils to learn how this information is *organised* – to perceive its structure. This is the *information structure* with which we are concerned here.

We can think of the information structure of a text as a meaning framework or, to use a term widely employed in psychology, as a 'frame'.[2] As used by psychologists the term 'frame' refers to a framework or structure which is used to make sense of the world (and of new information). Different frames are used for making sense of different situations or different types of information. So the information structures which we propose underlie science texts can be thought of as a specific subset of a more general set of frames used for making sense of new information.

The notion of structure carries with it the notion of *parts*, or *constituents*, even where these are abstract entities of some sort; likewise a frame can be thought of as having certain obligatory slots.

**Thus we can say that the information structure of a given text is defined by its information constituents.**

## Information constituents

By information constituents we mean something like elements of content – the sorts of things we expect the text to be about; the information slots we expect to be filled.[3] But we are not referring to specific subject matter. This is one reason why we feel it necessary to use a term other than content elements.

**We can think of information constituents as general classes or categories into which we might slot specific items of subject matter.**

For instance, in one text giving instructions to experiment, the apparatus might include *bunsen burners* and *test tubes*; in another, an *electric circuit* and *switches*. Bunsen burners, test tubes, circuits and switches are specific items of content; but conceptually we can classify them all as 'apparatus': it is the notion of 'apparatus' which is the *information constituent*. And it is the fact that where we find apparatus, we also expect to find 'materials', 'procedures or steps', 'results', and 'interpretation', that gives rise to the notion of information structure.

We expect to find certain information constituents in certain texts, and we expect these constituents to go together in ways which reflect what happens in the real world. This going-together of related information constituents contributes to the *coherence* or sense of a text. The absence of a key information constituent can destroy coherence, as can the insertion into the text of elements from alien structures.

The notion of structure as used here has its parallel in the physical world; scientists and geographers are also concerned with structures, albeit of a physical kind. Thus one of the information structures which underlies many texts in science and geography is that representing a *physical structure* of some kind. Just as information structures are made up of constituents, physical structures consist of *parts*.

For instance, in the 'Tooth structure' text we examined in the Introduction, there were references to the crown, the neck and the root of the tooth. The latter are specific items of content, but conceptually we can classify them as *parts* of a *physical structure*. The generality of the term 'information constituents' may be further illustrated by thinking of a geography text in which the structure of a suspension bridge is described.

Here we would expect to find references to the deck, the cables, the anchor points, and so on. Again these are specific items of content, but as related items of information they can also be classified as the 'parts of a structure'. And where the information constituent 'parts' is present, so too will be the constituents *properties*, *location*, and *function*.

The occurrence of this particular structure in geography and history as well as in science texts enables us to identify similarities as well as differences amongst texts across the curriculum.

In illustrating the notion of information structure we have identified two distinct structures underlying different types of science, and other texts: *instruction* and *physical structure*. This is a first step towards describing variations in science texts which is followed up in detail in Chapter 4.

We now use the notions of writer intention and information structure to examine text variation across the curriculum.

The distinction between English and science texts is sharpest and will serve to illustrate the distinctions we wish to draw out.

## Comparing the texts of science and English: writer intention

With the exception of poetry and passages specially selected for particular exercises, most English texts are *narrative*; science texts and many texts in the humanities used in schools are *informative*: they are expository or instructional. These general terms do not tell us anything about particular writer intentions; but they do point to the wider purposes of the different types of text.

We might say that the general function of narrative texts is to tell a story; in practice, things are much more complex than this. The novel or short story may well be thought of as an end in itself. Nevertheless, its story-telling function differentiates it, at the most fundamental level, from texts written for the purpose of informing: describing or explaining the real world, or instructing the reader in a particular procedure.

The narrative texts studied in English all share certain quite consistent features:

1. they all tell a story, ie they are structured by a story 'frame';
2. they are frequently written by professional writers;
3. they make reference to the personal rather than the public;
4. they are not intended, in themselves, to be 'educative'.

The texts which are used in science are all written for quite specific pedagogic purposes, but these purposes are manifold. While the instruction texts of science, like the narrative texts of English, do have consistent features in common, informative texts do not. For instance, an informative text which introduces a theory is as different from an informative text which describes a mechanism as it is from a narrative. Reading in science, we suggest, is more demanding than reading in English because it requires, as a basic condition, a willingness and capacity to deal with a wider range of text types.

## Meaning or information constituents

**The meaning constituents of the narrative are familiar, in principle, to all readers: the characters or actors around which a story revolves, their qualities and goals, the settings in which they find themselves, and the events and resolutions which result. The information constituents of informative texts, by contrast, vary widely according to the topic of the text.**

Thus, while texts giving *instructions* to experiment may all share the constituents – 'apparatus', 'materials' and 'steps' – texts describing a *theory* will have different constituents; and these will further differ from those describing *structures* or *processes*.

It is this wide variation in the basic constituents of science texts which, as we show in Chapter 4, gives rise to information structures which are not as familiar to readers as the story structure.

## Meaning or information structure

The structure of the story has been widely investigated by linguists and psychologists in recent years. They have been able to show how implicit knowledge of this structure serves as a framework for understanding; and that a knowledge of the basic structure of the story is acquired by children at an early age.

By contrast, the structure of expository and instructional texts has not been widely investigated, and the models which have been proposed are very tentative. More importantly, it seems likely that pupils coming to the task of reading in science do not bring with them the implicit knowledge of the structures of science texts that they have of the narrative. This is one reason why the reading demands of the text used in science and English are quite different.

## Reading demands of texts in science and English

Narrative text is conducive to the kind of reading termed *receptive reading* by the 'Effective Use of Reading' team. The reader who reads receptively is metaphorically carried along by the text, or, if you like, by a story framework; s/he is so involved that s/he is likely in fact to be unconscious of what s/he is doing.

Receptive reading may be contrasted with *reflective reading*. When reading reflectively the reader does actually break the flow of his or her progress through the text and reflect on something s/he has read about or related to what s/he is reading about. Reflective reading may well occur in reading narrative prose; indeed it is an essential requirement for the advanced study of literature – but it is not an essential requirement for the reading of narrative.

Both receptive and reflective reading play a part in learning from text but they make very different demands on the reader:

1. Receptive reading, by virtue of the fact that it is intrinsically rewarding, maintains motivation and generates interest in a topic or theme;
2. Reflective reading results in learning and in this respect may also be regarded as potentially rewarding;
3. Reflective reading is harder work – and it is the predominant demand of reading expository instructional texts;
4. Whereas (most) narrative texts offer the reader the option of reading receptively or reflectively, and we assume that some readers do pace themselves in this way, expository and instructional texts do not. Non-narrative prose does not offer the same opportunities for gear-changing.

The opportunities to read receptively are rare in science, so it is essential that reflective reading is rewarded by understanding. But this does not happen unless the reader knows when and where to stop and reflect. Knowing when and where to break reading for reflection is facilitated by knowledge of structure. The question is, do pupils coming to the task of learning from the expository and instructional texts of science possess even implicitly this knowledge? Our view is that they do not.

Without this knowledge, and the support and guidance from teachers who know the nature of the task, pupil reading in science is unlikely to be truly reflective, and is likely in fact to become rejective.

*Rejective reading*, as the term implies, is manifest either in a rejection of the task and the text, or in a passive passing over of print which does not result in satisfaction or learning. We know from personal experience when we ourselves respond rejectively to print, and we also know, from experience, the sort of texts which are likely to give rise to this reaction.

We doubt whether we are always as sensitive to the potential responses of our pupils. It is true that we have all encountered some pupils who manifest, even in junior school, the motivation to read widely about science and the flexibility and capacity to deal effectively with a wide range of types of text. These pupils seem to possess an implicit knowledge of information structuring from an early age and use it to pace their reading: they cope with new content and terminology with ease. Perhaps these are the students who go on to become great scientists or science teachers. They are, nevertheless, in the minority. For most pupils, reading in science is probably one of the most challenging demands made on them throughout their secondary schooling.

**If pupils are to be encouraged to maintain a lively interest in science beyond the novelty of experimental work in the first years of secondary schooling they will need to read, and read effectively.**

This, we believe, will not come about unless science teachers are prepared to provide support and guidance in reading throughout the secondary school. Because the demands of reading in science are subject-specific they cannot be met by 'reading' or 'skills' lessons which go on elsewhere in the curriculum. The responsibility for training must be in the hands of the experts in science – the science teachers.

## Summary

In our discussion of the nature of reading in science we have tried to suggest some starting points for providing support and guidance for our pupils.

*1.* We propose that a first step is to concentrate on the content and structure of texts used in science, rather than on features like terminology. In effect we are saying that if we take care of content and structure, terminology will look after itself. This we will illustrate in the next section.
*2.* We have said, however, that we have much to learn about structure, but have pointed to some quite fundamental differences between the structure of the narrative texts of English and the instructional and expository texts of science.
*3.* We have also tried to show that pupils have an advantage in reading narrative, namely possession of the story framework, but lack the counterpart(s) of this structure when they come to read science texts.
*4.* A further challenge of reading in science is that pupils have to deal with a range of different text types, with unfamiliar and extensive content.
*5.* Three kinds of reading response have been discussed: receptive, reflective and rejective.
*6.* It has been asserted that the opportunities for reading receptively are rare in science. Teachers will themselves consider whether or where there is a place for provision of material which will give rise to receptive reading.

Our concern is to indicate ways in which the reflective reading required for most science texts will be rewarding. This is the question to which we turn in the next section, where we describe some techniques which provide support and guidance for pupil reading.

## Notes

1. The terms 'meaning' and 'information' are used synonymously, but we have adopted the convention of using the term 'meaning' when referring to narrative texts, and 'information' when referring to non-narrative texts.
2. The terms 'structure' and 'frame' are from now on used interchangeably; but the term 'structure' is generally preferred when the focus is on the text and the term 'frame' when it is on the learner.
3. The terms 'slot' and 'constituent' are used interchangeably.

# 3
# Towards Effective Reading in Science

## A rationale for directed activities related to text

The objective of these activities is to encourage active reflective reading. Current theory predicts that learning from text is furthered by reflection, ideally by reflection which occurs at critical points in the text. These critical points vary from text to text and with different purposes, but generally speaking they should focus attention on information constituents or the relations between constituents.

How do we plan reading activities which encourage our pupils to break their reading at these salient points and attend to these constituents and relations?

### Providing specific instructions

First, we give specific rather than general instructions to our readers. *General instructions* are instructions like:
'Read (for homework) and make notes.'
'Learn what's in that chapter for a test.'
'Read and pick out the main points.'
*Specific instructions* on the other hand, might be something like:
'Find and mark all the references to lead bromide.'
'Underline in red all the words or phrases which refer to the parts of the electric bell.'
'Label the parts on the diagram.'
The differences between the general and the specific instructions are:

*1.* the general instruction gives no indication to the learner of how to go about the reading task;
*2.* it gives no clues about the relative importance of the different elements of content;
*3.* it does not require the learner to break his or her read or to reflect at critical points.

It is not surprising that pupils who are given a general instruction 'blindly copy'. With respect to guidance in the nature of the task they are blind. Furthermore, the teacher who gives the general instruction does not need to know what is in the text – indeed the instruction may be given without the teacher reading the text at all.

By contrast, the teacher who gives a specific instruction does need to know what is in the text and will have made some judgement about the relative importance of the different constituents.

**Directed activities related to text are all activities which involve the provision of specific instructions to pupils.**

The specific instructions are intended to realise two objectives. First, in the short run, they are intended to break the reading of a particular text at the points where the teacher decides reflection ought to go on – and hence to facilitate learning of the content of that text. Second, they are intended to give pupils practice in active reading and experience of feeling their way into the structure of different texts – the aim is that such experience will be transferred to their own independent study.

One very important feature of providing specific instructions is that they are instructions which can be followed. They put pupils in problem-solving situations and create opportunities for reflective reading to be rewarded.

### Providing opportunities for feedback

We can think of the rewards of reflective reading in terms of feedback. Feedback for the reader on his or her interpretation of written material is regarded as essential in learning. Unlike the listener in a conversation, who can ask the speaker questions if s/he does not understand, the silent solitary reader of text does not have direct access to the writer. On the other hand s/he can go back over the print and approach difficult bits from alternative angles. When s/he is working at the text in a problem-solving way with a teacher or other pupils, s/he can also make use of their interpretations.

**Directed reading activities are designed to make use of two sources of feedback: the text itself and other readers.**

Pupils are encouraged to discuss their findings and to check their hypotheses against the text.

**Pupils whose reading is directed in the ways outlined above are active learners, and the activity in which they engage is not unscientific.**

We think of the texts that pupils work on as sets of data or phenomena which may be analysed, reflected upon, and classified in much the same way as any other data or phenomena.

The activity often takes the form of physical manipulation or marking of the text. Like many other practical activities in science, it is frequently, though not always, followed by a recording outcome. Outcomes are also specific to the text and the task, unlike the general instruction 'read and make notes'. Frequently, the recording task requires pupils to complete or construct a table or diagram.

**The form of recording which is chosen should reflect the nature of the content and the text.**

For instance, when the text is about the classification of phenomena, a table or hierarchical diagram may be asked for; if the content describes a process, a flow chart may be more appropriate.

## Summary

Directed reading activities involve specific instructions designed to help pupils to pause and reflect in their reading and to *locate important information*. They involve pupils *in categorising* information, and *in recording* it in a way which reflects the information structure of the text.

A list of the principal reading activities developed by the 'Reading for Learning' project is presented on page 48.

## The directed activities related to text

### How do they work?

The directed reading activities are designed to focus attention on text. They direct pupil attention by making pupils focus on important parts of the text, and by involving them in reflecting on the content of the text. As we have seen already, the reading activities involve pupils in discussion, in sharing, and in revising their interpretations.

The reading activities fall into two broad categories:

### Reconstruction or completion activities

These are essentially *problem-solving* activities. They make use of *modified text*. The text or diagram has parts missing: words, phrases or labels are deleted, or, alternatively, the text is broken into segments which have to be re-ordered or re-arranged.

The activities have *game-like* characteristics. The game involves hunting for clues in order to complete the text. Attention is focused because there is a problem to be solved. Some, but not all, clues are available.

There is satisfaction and reward. Attention is directed because the content of the text has to be taken into account if the game is to be played properly.

*Table 4 Directed activities related to text*

| Reconstruction activities (using text modified by teacher) | Analysis activities (using straight text) |
|---|---|
| *Pupil task*: pupils *complete text* or diagram, *reconstructing meaning*. | *Pupil task*: Pupils locate and categorise text information by marking and labelling. Use marked text as basis for summary (diagrammatic or note form). |

Reconstruction activities:

1. *Text completion*
   (a) Word completion (selected words deleted from text).
   (b) Phrase completion (selected phrases/clauses deleted from text).
   (c) Sentence completion (selected sentences deleted from text).

2. *Sequencing*
   (a) scrambled segments of text arranged in logical/time sequence (text cut into segments representing steps/events etc).
   (b) Segments of text classified (texts cut into segments representing certain categories of information).

3. *Prediction*
   (a) Pupils predict next event/step or stage after reading segments of text (text segments presented a section at a time).
   (b) Pupils write next part or end of text (text presented a section at a time).

4. *Table completion*
   (a) Pupils fill in cells of table using row and column headings and text as sources of information. (Teacher provides row and column headings.)
   (b) Pupils devise row and column headings using texts and cells of matrix as sources of information. (Teacher fills in cells.)

5. *Diagram completion*
   (a) Label completion using text and diagram as sources of information (selected labels deleted from diagrams).
   (b) Diagram completion using text and partly complete diagram as sources of information. (Teacher constructs original diagram: flow diagram, branching tree, network, etc.)

Analysis activities:

1. *Text marking*
   Locating and underlining parts of text representing certain meaning of information targets.

2. *Labelling*
   Pupils label parts of text using labels provided by teacher.

3. *Segmenting*
   Pupils break text into meaning or information units and label/annotate segments of text.

4. *Table construction*
   Pupils produce column and row headings for tables and fill in cells using text(s) as source of information.

5. *Diagram construction*
   Pupils construct and complete diagram appropriate for particular text, eg *flow diagram* for text describing a process, *branching tree* for a text describing a hierarchical classification, networks, etc.

6. *Pupil-generated questions*
   Pupils read text and generate questions they still need answers to.

7. *Summary*
   Pupils produce headings and summarise information.

**Analysis activities**

These do not require that the text be modified. So *straight text* is used.

The activities are, on the surface, more *study-like* than game-like. The aim of the activities is to find particular meaning or information 'targets' in the text. The teacher decides what the information constituents of the text are; s/he decides which of these to focus on. S/he gives labels to the information constituents; these are the text targets which pupils are going to search for. Searching for the targets involves pupils in locating and categorising the information in the text.

Again, this study is facilitated by discussion with one or two other pupils.

When the targets are found they are marked by underlining and/or by labelling.

The search for targets is followed by a class discussion in which the merits of alternative markings are considered and pupils have a further opportunity to modify or revise their judgements.

**Analysis reading activities, we believe, have greater potential for transfer by pupils to their own independent study than do reconstruction reading activities.**

Reconstruction reading activities, on the other hand, are initially more motivating and should feed-in to pupil writing of more extended text than do analysis activities. Analysis activities lead to a more condensed representation of text 'information'.

# In practice

### 1. Materials

The selection of texts for directed reading activities is made by the teacher.

**Texts are always those which would be used in the ongoing context of the curriculum and in the light of knowledge about pupils.**

In preparing for the activities, the general practice is to ensure that all pupils have a copy of the text to be studied. This is particularly important if the reading activity involves the pupils directly in locating and marking important elements of content. Teachers should be careful to obtain copyright permission from the publishers. (See notes on obtaining copyright permission on pages vi and 144.)

Copies of the text used for a directed reading activity may make up a set which is used by different groups of pupils, or they may be filed by individual pupils after the directed reading activity and kept as a personal record of the work done. Where copies make up a set we suggest that they are protected by plastic or acetate covers, or inserted into plastic envelopes. Any marking of the text can then be done on the cover in washable pens and subsequently erased. Alternatively, pupils may be provided with acetate sheets to lay over material which is going to be re-used.

In general, most of the teachers with whom we have worked prefer their pupils to keep copies of worked-over texts. These are useful both for revision of content and as exemplars of a method of text study. We like the idea of pupils being able to return to texts which they have, for instance, underlined and labelled, especially when a recording outcome of the text marking, like a diagram, is also included in the file.

## 2. Discussion

**Discussion is facilitated by the provision of a copy of each text to be used for each pupil involved, and by keeping group size to a minimum; pupils work in pairs or in groups of three.**

Only when the teacher and pupils are experienced in small group discussion does the size of the group increase. Furthermore, teachers experienced in working with mixed-ability classes usually ensure that weaker readers are paired with at least one more confident reader. In classes where there is a predominance of less-confident readers, pupils are often given the opportunity to follow the print while the teacher reads it aloud before the pupils undertake the reading task. Indeed, with almost all classes, the lesson begins with the teacher reading the text aloud while the pupils follow.

The discussion has a purpose. Pupils are expected to make decisions. They are also expected to revise their decisions in the light of further information. This is made available through the pooling of ideas in a teacher-led class discussion at the end of the lesson. The nature of the topic and of the text, as well as the teacher's own teaching style, determine the extent to which conclusions are open or closed. Frequently, though not always, a consensus is reached.

## 3. Observing pupil responses

Because the lesson has been very carefully planned, and because pupils are taking an active part in the lesson, it is possible for pupil performance to be closely monitored by the teacher.

**Insight into pupil interpretations may be gained from group and class discussions; and further evidence is available from marked-up texts as well as by recording outcomes.**

Pupils are also informed about the objectives of the lesson and are clear about what follow-up is required of them. The relevance of the reading activity for their homework and study is frequently discussed.

## Examples of directed-reading activities: reconstruction activities

### Completion

There follow three examples of completion activities.

### 1. Text completion: prediction of words deleted on a regular basis

This is the activity known as *cloze procedure*. Originally developed as a technique for assessing the readability of texts, it is also used as a test of comprehension.

**When used as a directed-reading activity, deletion serves to initiate discussion and reflection about the important concepts and language of the text.**

Words are deleted from the text to leave gaps. Gaps are usually of uniform size so that clues to the word are drawn from the meaning of the text, rather than from 'letter clues' or word shape.

   An example of text prepared for cloze by the deletion of every fifth word is shown below.

---

**Modified text 1: Expansion and contraction of solids**

Materials expand when they are heated. Most materials expand, or become larger, when they are heated, and contract, or become smaller, when they are cooled. The expansion of solid materials, like iron and brass, is so small that it is not noticed unless special apparatus is used to measure it and to show that it is, in fact, occurring.

   The expansion of solids. Push the metal ball of a ball and ring apparatus through the ring. Heat the ball and, when it is red hot, lift it with tongs and place it on the ring. The ball does not fall through the ring. It has expanded. What happens when the ball cools and contracts?

   Heat the bar of a bar and guage apparatus. Try to push the bar into the guage. It does not fit. Allow the bar to cool. It now fits into the guage for it has contracted in length.

   Lay a thick iron rod across two bricks. Use Plasticine to attach a straw to one end of a knitting needle. Place the needle, so that the straw is upright, on one of the bricks and underneath the rod. Then

---

heat the rod. The straw turns. Why? Now allow the rod to cool. The straw now turns in the opposite direction. Why?

Expansion and contraction can _____ a nuisance or even _____ damage. Therefore, engineers make _____ for expansion and contraction. _____ pipes are built with _____ , bends and moveable collars _____ that no damage is _____ when the pipes become _____ and expand. Telephone wires _____ power cables are left _____ so they do not _____ when they contract in _____ weather. Large metal bridges _____ loosely on rollers or _____ pads built into their _____ .

Then expansion can take place freely and no damage is done to the bridges. Narrow tar-filled gaps are sometimes made in concrete roads so that cracking does not occur when the concrete expands. The rails on a railway track are welded together to make a single rail that is often more than one kilometre in length. This rail is heated and stretched. It is then fixed down firmly in the expanded state so that it contracts only slightly when the weather becomes colder. The pendulums of clocks are sometimes provided with wooden or plastic bobs and adjustable nuts. Wood and plastic do not expand as much as metals. The nut of a pendulum is turned so that the position of the bob is altered and allowance made for expansion and contraction.

From C. Windridge, *General Science*, Book 1.

## 2. Text completion: words deleted on an irregular basis

**While we believe that pupil discussion based on cloze passages deleted on a regular basis does have some potential for learning, we consider that an irregular or selective system of deletion has greater potential.**

A selective pattern of deletion is illustrated below.

### Modified text 2: making allowances for expansion and contraction

Expansion and contraction can be a nuisance or even cause damage. Therefore, engineers make allowances for expansion and contraction. Steam pipes are built with loops, bends and moveable collars so that no damage is done when the pipes become hot and expand. Telephone wires and power cables are left slack so they do not snap when they contract in cold weather. Large metal bridges rest _____ on rollers or plastic pads built into their supports.

Then _____ can take place freely and no _____ is done to the bridges. Narrow tar-filled _____ are sometimes made in concrete roads so that _____ does not occur when the concrete expands. The rails on a railway track are welded together to make a _____ rail that is often

---

more than one kilometre in length. This rail is heated and stretched. It is then fixed down firmly in the _____ state so that it contracts only slightly when the weather becomes _____ . The pendulums of clocks are sometimes provided with wooden or plastic bobs and adjustable nuts. _____ and plastic do not expand as much as _____ . The nut of a pendulum is turned so that the position of the bob is altered and allowance made for expansion and contraction.

From C. Windridge, *General Science*, Book 1.

---

With a regular system of deletion, 1 in 10, 1 in 7, 1 in 5, the teacher has little control over what aspects of content or of language are focused on. When deletion is selective there is much greater control, since the teacher decides what words will be deleted.

A comparison of the two 'Expansion' examples serves to illustrate this. The comparison is best undertaken through reference to the deleted words listed below.

| *Example 1* | *Example 2* |
|---|---|
| *Regular deletion* | *Selected deletion* |
| be | loosely |
| cause | expansion |
| allowances | damage |
| steam | gaps |
| loops | cracking |
| so | single |
| done | expanded |
| rest | colder |
| plastic | wood |
| supports | metals |

Of the ten gaps in Example 1, five can be filled by words (either the original – 'be', 'cause', 'so', 'done', and 'rest' – or synonyms) purely on the basis of language cues. No reference to the content of the passage is required and hence in discussions about clozing the gaps there is unlikely to be reference to the important concepts discussed in the passage. The remaining five gaps, by contrast, do require reference to the content of the text. But there is a sense in which they also require reference *outside* the text. There is not enough information left in the text for 'good' predictions about appropriate words to be made. There is no way of knowing in advance, for instance, that the example of allowances for expansion cited by the writer will be 'steam' pipes, nor of knowing in advance that 'loops' as well as bends will be built in. In sum, deletions may not be sufficiently demanding of effort, or irrelevant to the content, or they may be too demanding.

When the teacher is selective about deletions there is a greater chance, though not a certainty, that the essential concepts or language will be focused on. The 'gaps' in example 2 are intended to get pupils to reflect upon:

1. means of allowing for expansion, as in
   bridges resting *loosely*
   concrete roads having *gaps*
2. the effects of expansion and contraction, as in
   causing *damage*, and
   roads *cracking*
3. the application of knowledge about expansion, as in
   making a *single* rail
   fixed in its *expanded* state
   contraction occuring in *colder* weather

and so on. Furthermore, use can be made of the information in the un-deleted text. The task is therefore one which encourages reflection and the use of information in the text.

### 3. Completion of text and/or diagram when these are related

Completion activities may be based not only on texts in which words have been deleted, but also on texts in which *phrases* or *sentences* have been deleted (examples of such activities may be found in *Learning from the Written Word*). However, one of the most widely used completion activities in science lessons is *diagram* completion.

In the example below, words have been deleted from text, but the text is supported by a diagram. Pupils use the information given in the diagram to complete the text; then they use the text information to annotate the diagram. Alternatively, they could have been presented with the complete text and been asked to *label* the diagram from which labels had been deleted.

---

**Modified text 3: the eye**

The light from something you look at goes into the eye through a small hole called the _____ . The light is made to bend by the _____ and a _____ . They *focus* it into the back of the eye where it forms an *image*.

We *see* the image because the back of the eye is a kind of black screen (called the _____ ) that senses light. It is covered with nerve cells that react when light reaches them and send a message along the _____ to the brain.

---

At a place where the main optic nerve leaves the eye there are no cells that can sense light. This makes a _____ . If light strikes here we cannot sense it!

If too much light meets the retina the cells can be damaged. So in bright light the coloured ring of muscle in the eye (the ___ ) gets bigger. This cuts down the amount of light that can get through the _____ .

To get the light to focus in the right place, the lens has to be the right shape. When you focus on something near you the lens has to be fat; for something far away it has to be thin. The _____ holding the lens in place does this by squeezing or stretching the lens.

From a text produced by a teacher group

Instructions to pupils were:

*1.* Read the passage below this carefully. Some words are missing from it. All the words you need are on the diagram of the eye. Discuss with your neighbour which is the right word for each gap, then fill in the gap.

*2.* When you have done this, write a few words alongside each label on the diagram of the eye, explaining what the job of that part of the eye is in helping you to see something.

**Figure 1**

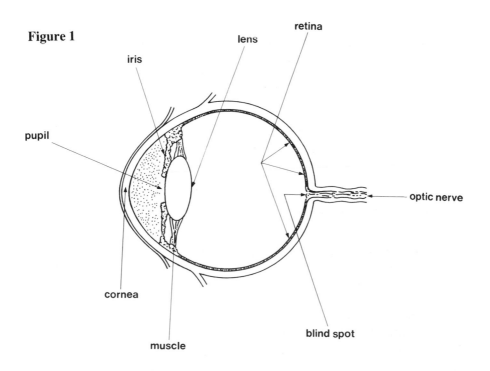

An example of one pupil's annotation of the diagram is given below:

**Figure 2**

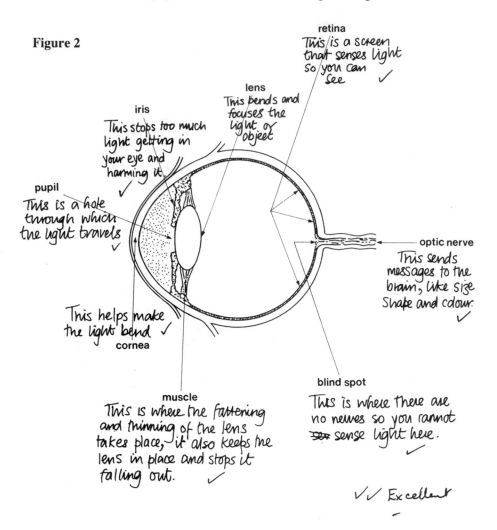

retina
This is a screen
that senses light
so you can
see ✓

lens
This bends and
focuses the
light or
object

iris
This stops too much
light getting in
your eye and
harming it ✓

pupil
This is a hole
through which
the light travels ✓

optic nerve
This sends
messages to the
brain, like size
shape and colour. ✓

This helps make
the light bend ✓
cornea

muscle
This is where the flattening
and thinning of the lens
takes place, it also keeps the
lens in place and stops it
falling out. ✓

blind spot
This is where there are
no nerves so you cannot
see sense light here. ✓

✓✓ Excellent

The potential of the completion activities illustrated here is that they involve pupils in a close study of the information left in the text, and in the
use of contextual clues. For this reason, the completion activities of the
project must be distinguished from 'tests' which involve 'filling the gaps' or
selecting the right word from a list. The use of contextual clues is, however,
dependent upon the provision of a context: when there is no supporting
diagram, this involves providing a lead-in of at least a paragraph in which
there are no deletions. Similarly, it is also helpful to leave a paragraph or
more without deletions at the end, and to encourage pupils to search this,
as well as the lead-in, for clues.

Furthermore, completion activities are not intended to be isolated solitary exercises: they involve discussion of alternatives in pairs or small groups and a pooling of ideas in a teacher-led class discussion at the end of the lesson. Time has to be allowed for this, as well as for the activity. If the activity is to occupy, say, a forty-five minute period, it is unlikely that pupils will close more than ten gaps, though this will depend upon the extent to which pupils are prepared to discuss possibilities. This in turn is determined in part by the nature of the gaps. The greater the number of possibilities the greater the opportunity for discussion.

Finally, the success or failure of completion reading activities is very largely dependent on the *teacher's judgement* about what words to delete. This is dependent upon both the lesson objectives and on the text itself. So it is not possible to suggest simple rules for the deletion of any given text – these must be judged by the teacher him- or herself through trial and error. On the other hand we can offer some guidelines as to when and how to use deletion. Thus, if the objective is to focus on *concepts (and/or terminology)* the deletion pattern is one which encourages pupils to consider alternative concepts for each gap. If the objective is to focus pupil attention on *related concepts* then the deletion pattern will be one in which some of the words or phrases showing relations are left in, and some are deleted. If the objective is to focus pupil attention on *principles* or on *the structure of the text as a whole* a limited number of phrases or sentences, as opposed to words, can be deleted.

### Sequencing of scrambled text

For a sequencing activity the text is modified by being cut into segments. The pupil task is to arrange the segments in the order which makes the most sense.

**The objective of sequencing is to sort out information according to logical or linguistic criteria.**

Logical criteria predominate in content areas, linguistic in English.

Pupils work in twos or threes with the segments of the text which has been cut up. Ideally segments should be equally spaced out on the sheet before cutting up, as shown in the example on page 58 (in which numbers are in scrambled sequence). This helps to prevent the loss of smaller strips of paper and makes cutting up and packaging easier.

It must be emphasised that the physical manipulation of the actual segments of text is an essential feature of sequencing. It provides for feedback

*4.* Collect a piece of Plasticine, a measuring cylinder, and a beaker

*3.* Make the Plasticine into a box shape

*7.* Fill the measuring cylinder with water up to the 50 $cm^3$ volume mark

*1.* Carefully slide the Plasticine into the water without making a splash

*5.* Read off the new volume in the measuring cylinder

*2.* Empty the measuring cylinder and dry the Plasticine

*8.* Roll the Plasticine into a long thin sausage. Be sure to use all the Plasticine that was in the block

*10.* Fill the measuring cylinder with water up to the 50 $cm^3$ volume mark

*6.* Carefully slide the Plasticine sausage into the water. Note: all the Plasticine should be under the water

*9.* Read off the volume in the measuring cylinder

From D. Tinbergen and P. Thorburn, *Wreake Valley Integrated Science Project*, Book 1.

to pupils on their preliminary choices in a way that just looking at dis-ordered segments in print does not.

The decision about where to cut a text is made by the teacher after analysing the text; it may or may not coincide with paragraph segments. It depends upon the sort of problem the teacher wishes to set. The size of unit for sequencing also depends upon teacher objectives, and the text: the sentence is usually the smallest unit of text used with science texts.

Since the task of sequencing involves pupils using logical or time clues, it follows that it is useful for getting pupils to sort out the steps of an experiment in advance or to overlearn the stages in a process or life cycle. The activity has been widely and successfully used by science teachers for these purposes, especially as a preparation for experimental work.

## Reconstruction activities: summary

Four examples of reconstruction activities have been presented: word completion, diagram completion, and sequencing. Further examples of sequencing, table and diagram completion are given in Chapter 5. For a more comprehensive account of the use of the different reconstruction activities in subjects across the curriculum, the reader is referred to *Learning from the Written Word.*

Notes on the potential of each activity and practical considerations to be borne in mind are given below. These are in the form of notes summarising the potential of each activity as a learning activity and the practical considerations which need to be borne in mind when selecting and designing the reading activities.

# 1. Text completion

**Potential**

*1.* Text completion is motivating because some resolution of the problem is always possible.

2. It is game-like, hence useful for beginning study skills and for younger pupils.

*3.* It also encourages reflection on concepts and over-learning of terminology (even with sixth form).

*4.* It should feed in to writing.

*5.* It involves pupils in decision-making and identifying criteria for decision-making.

**Considerations**

*1.* Text completion directs attention to text structure indirectly, so objective should be to focus on structure at end of exercise, say in the plenary session.

2. When making deletions, it is important to bring out relations amongst deletions.

*3.* The choice of unit for deletion, eg word, phrase, or sentence, is determined by text and purpose of activity.

*4.* Responses of pupils may be unpredictable; for instance, they may focus on grammatical constraints as opposed to logical clues.

*5.* Too many deletions will result in a task which is difficult or boring.

6. Lead-in should always be provided and perhaps one example done as a class activity.

*7.* Discussion of alternatives amongst pairs or groups is essential.

*8.* In class discussion, criteria for choice should be made explicit and class choices compared with original text.

## 2. Sequencing and prediction

### Potential

*1.* Sequencing and prediction focus attention on procedural, or logical order, and/or on materials/apparatus for an experiment and/or on necessary precautions.
*2.* Ideally, they involve pupils in thinking about the purpose of an experiment before doing it, and in rehearsing procedures.
*3.* Sequencing a process or life cycle gives pupils the opportunity actively to rehearse the stages and relate them to each other.

### Considerations

*1.* In sequencing, segments need to be cut at points which coincide with step or stage or logical section.
*2.* In sequencing, if too many language cues are given in the text, eg 'first', 'second', and so on, pupils may ignore logical cues.
*3.* An over-used activity could become stale and an end in itself.
*4.* Sequencing requires care and time in practical preparation: making sure that segments are the same size and that cuts are straight to avoid providing 'cutting clues'.
*5.* In sequencing, choice has to be made between presenting segments which are then ordered and stuck in books, or presenting segments on plastic-covered card which may be re-used with other classes.

## 3. Table completion

### Potential

*1.* Table completion provides experience in the use and construction of tables and gives pupils a 'model' of this form of summary.
*2.* It is essential, therefore, as a foundation for table construction.
*3.* It involves active classification of information and brings out dimensions of classification.
*4.* It is almost obligatory, therefore, for texts which give details of classification systems but may be used with all types of text.
*5.* Table completion provides an ideal format for summarising the information structure of the text; column or row headings are frequently based on information constituents of a text.
*6.* In fact, it has the widest application of all the reading activities and for all types of text.

7. It is suitable for use with pupils at all levels of secondary schooling and for primary school children.

8. It provides a useful summary for revision purposes.

9. It provides an information base for writing summaries and notes and is therefore an alternative to 'copying': empty cells are as informative as entries and provide stimulus for further research.

10. When preceded by underlining and labelling, it may be done for homework.

### Considerations

1. Table completion requires the teacher to do prior analysis of the text and to construct a skeleton table and to provide some, if not all, column and row headings.

2. It should always be preceded by underlining and labelling.

3. It requires discussion with pupils on dimensions of classification and perhaps, if possible, column and row headings.

## 4. Diagram and label completion: analogues (ie semi-pictorial representations of structures, mechanisms, etc)

### Potential

1. Diagram and label completion break the reading of the text at specified critical points for focus onto diagram.

2. They result in active use of diagram and text, and learning of parts and location.

3. The focus may also be on function of parts and on relating process to structure.

4. Techniques may be introduced *before* using or studying actual mechanism, to facilitate handling, or *after*, as a means of revision.

5. If used regularly, the techniques should quickly be transferred to pupils' own study and increase confidence in dealing with structure/mechanism texts.

6. They may be used for homework.

7. Annotated diagrams may be used for revision.

### Considerations

1. If activity is to be self-correcting, *information to be used in labelling diagram must be available in the text*, otherwise the activity is a test, not a learning exercise.

2. The diagram to be labelled should be presented on a separate sheet so that diagrams and text can be referred to simultaneously.

3. The diagram on a separate sheet also makes annotation and labelling easier.

4. Feedback should be provided so that pupils end up with correct labelling. Use of overhead transparencies will enable pupils to do own corrections with teacher checking individual work.

## 5. Diagram completion: flow diagrams, hierarchies

### Potential

1. Diagram completion of flow diagrams and hierarchies provides experience of 'models' of different information structures.

2. It involves active classification of information.

3. It provides a powerful and useful format for revision purposes.

4. It provides an information base for writing summaries and notes and is an alternative to 'copying'.

### Considerations

1. This type of diagram completion usually requires the teacher to do a 'model' first, which needs experience, and perhaps consultation with colleagues.

2. Decisions about what parts of 'model' diagram to delete require flexibility and knowledge of pupils.

3. In general, greater support (and fewer deletions) are provided for less confident pupils, less support and more skeletal diagram for the more confident.

4. Diagram completion should be preceded by underlining/labelling of elements to be represented.

5. Pupils should be involved in discussion about different ways of representing information and encouraged to evaluate alternatives.

6. The selection of a diagrammatic form is determined by the nature of the text.

7. Flow diagrams are appropriate for process texts and for texts in which sequences are represented.

8. A particular form of the flow diagram which we will call *parallel listing* is useful for representing parallel processes or states of equilibrium.

9. Hierarchies and branching trees are appropriate for representing classifications of various kinds and are hence used with classification texts.

See also *Learning from the Written Word* Part 1, Section B.

## Examples of directed reading activities – analysis activities

The objective of analysis-reading activities is to focus attention on one or more information constituents of a text during a single reading session. The teacher analyses the text in the first instance to decide what information constituents are to be the focus of attention; for example, 'features' or 'properties' of a phenomenon; 'stages' in a process; 'evidence' of one kind or another, and so on.

### 1. Text marking

Pupils work in pairs to find and underline those parts of the text related to the target set by the teacher. An example of pupil underlining of a text is illustrated below:

---

**Text 1: Gravity**

Over 300 years ago, a young man named Isaac Newton was sitting in the garden of his home in Lincolnshire. Suddenly, as he was sitting there thinking, an apple dropped from a tree and fell to the ground. Newton started to wonder why an apple, when it was no longer held to the tree, should fall to the ground. Why did it not, for example, 'fall to the sky'? Why the ground? Could there be something about the Earth which was pulling the apple to it?

It was this idea that led Newton to make his discovery of the law of gravitation. He worked out that not only was the Earth pulling the apple, but that to a far lesser extent the apple was pulling on the Earth. In fact gravity is the force that tends to pull all bodies together. The more massive the body, the stronger its gravity. When the apple broke away from the tree, the Earth pulled upon the apple, and at the same time the apple tried to pull the Earth up to meet it. But an apple being so tiny compared with the Earth, it was only the apple that could be seen to move.

Gravity affects everything and everyone all the time. It is the reason why a book will fall to the ground when you knock it off a table, and why the water will run out of a bath when you take away the plug. The Earth is tending to pull everything downwards towards its centre. Therefore, if you stand on a high chair and jump outwards or even upwards, in fact you will not continue to go upwards or outwards because the Earth will be able to pull you downwards until you hit the hard ground again. The further you fall, the faster you will go, because gravity is pulling you all the time, and so your speed becomes greater and greater. (See Chapter 21)

Jump off a high wall, and you will land with a thump that may make

---

you sprain an ankle, because you will be moving much faster by the time that you reach the ground than if you had only jumped off a chair. But if you were to jump off a cliff, or from a high window, you would be moving so fast by the time you hit the ground that you might very likely be killed.          From C. Ronan, *Book of Science*.

How was the activity introduced? First, the text was analysed by the teacher in order to decide what the pupils' targets would be. This was an easy task since the text is a highly coherent piece of writing which clearly introduces a *concept* and a number of laws or *principles*, illustrated with examples. The concept is clearly signalled with a definition: 'In fact gravity is the force that tends to pull all bodies together.'

The targets pupils were to search for were the higher-order definitions and laws relating to the concept.

The method of locating the targets was underlining.

The instructions to pupils working in pairs were:

*1.* Read the text through to the end and then decide what basic message the writer is trying to get across, that is, what the most important 'message', 'principle', or 'idea' in the whole extract is. When you have agreed what this is, write your answer down.
*2.* Now find and underline no more than two sentences or parts of sentences which most clearly express this idea.

The sentences numbered 1 and 2 in the passage were the most popular choices. They were chosen by the majority of pupils. Next in popularity were sentences 3, 4 and 5.

In the class discussion which followed, all choices were justified. At the same time considerable controversy was generated by the phrase: 'downwards towards the centre'. A number of pupils argued that the term 'downwards' gave an erroneous notion of gravity, since it seemed to be counter to the idea that all bodies are exerting a gravitational pull regardless of their position in space. The question of a force that might act to reduce velocity was raised by the underlining of sentence 4.

We believe that in this activity, and in others involving underlining, pupils clearly demonstrate that they have the competence to locate the important parts of a text for the purposes of learning. The eleven- and twelve-year-olds who worked on the 'Gravity' text showed that they could distinguish between statements of principle and examples or illustrations. Furthermore, the activity has potential in concept learning, providing, as in this instance, an opportunity for a close examination of over-simplifications in the text.

The success of the task is, of course, dependent on the teacher's prior analysis of the text – on his or her judgement of what is important about it. From this starting point, represented in the task instructions, pupils are capable of working at the text independently of the teacher, gaining practice in focusing on one information constituent at a time.

**The concentration on one aspect of a text at a time involves pupils in a search for those parts of the text which are related to a particular information constituent, giving them practice in using a framework.**

These are the 'targets', being the parts of the text which are marked, most usually by underlining though there is no reason why other marking systems should not be adopted.

## 2. Text and diagram

In the second example of an analysis reading activity below, the targets are to be found in both text and diagram. In contrast to the gravity example, the task will involve pupils in an initial focus on lower-order units of information rather than high-order statements. This is a direct outcome of the difference between the two texts.

---

**Text 2: What happens during electrolysis?**

If we now consider the electrolysis of lead bromide we may be able to work out the sequence of events which ends with the production of lead and bromine.

We know that lead bromide is an ionic compound and that the solid form consists of a giant structure of lead and bromide ions. When we heat the solid it fuses (melts) and the strong bonds holding the ions in the crystal lattice are broken (Kinetic Theory, Section 1.3). Molten lead bromide is made up of lead ions, $Pb^{2+}$ and bromide ions, $Br^-$ all moving in a random fashion. Putting a pair of electrodes into the melt, however, seems to direct the movement of the ions. The electrodes are connected to a battery or other source of direct current and so electrons are being 'pumped' from the negative pole of the battery to the cathode. Because the electron flow enters the electrolyte at the cathode, it is negatively charged and another way of defining a cathode is to say that it is the electrode by which electrons enter an apparatus from an external circuit. The electrons cannot 'jump' across from the cathode to the anode and yet they must be continually leaving the cathode and arriving at the anode in order to return to the battery and complete the circuit. How are the moving ions connected with this electron flow? Why should the lead ions, $Pb^{2+}$, and the bromide ions, Br⁻, move towards the electrodes? Are they attracted to one electrode only or both?

We can answer all these questions by saying simply that 'opposite charges attract'. When the current is switched on and the electrons flow along the wire to the cathode, making it negatively charged, the positively charged lead ions are attracted to it and the negatively charged bromide ions are attracted to the positively charged anode. As each bromide ion reaches the anode it gives up an electron and becomes once again an atom of bromine:

$$Br^- \rightarrow Br + e^-$$

(Remember that bromide ions are formed when each bromine atom gains an electron; consequently when a bromide ion loses an electron to the anode it must become a bromine atom again.)

The bromine atoms join in pairs to form bromine molecules:

$$2Br \rightarrow Br_2(g)$$

and so bromine vapour is evolved.

The electron removed from the bromine ion is passed on through the carbon electrode and the copper connecting wire to the battery; thus the current is kept flowing.

At the cathode each lead ion receives two electrons from those flowing from the battery, through the connecting wire and the carbon rod, and so becomes a lead atom:

$$Pb^{2+} + 2e^- \rightarrow Pb(1)$$

The lead atoms bond together to form the giant structure of metallic lead.

During electrolysis, therefore, the ions are discharged and this giving of electrons to the ions by the cathode, and taking of electrons from the negatively charged ions by the anode, keeps the current flowing in the circuit. Within the electrolyte, however, the electrons are not handed on like buckets of water in a chain, as they are in metals, but are carried by the ions, which can be compared to one group of individuals taking full buckets of water from the tap to the fire and others taking empty ones back from the fire to the taps (13.3).

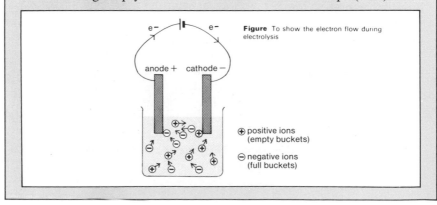

**Figure** To show the electron flow during electrolysis

⊕ positive ions (empty buckets)

⊖ negative ions (full buckets)

The ions which carry positive charges and which are therefore attracted to the cathode are called cations. Metal ions and hydrogen ions are cations. Anions are those ions carrying negative charges and are attracted to the anode: these are the ions of non-metals and of radicals such as sulphate, nitrate and carbonate.

From L. Davies, M. J. Denial, A. W. Locke and M. E. Reay,
*Investigating Chemistry*

This is a more complex text than the passage on gravity. It explains a general *process* – that of electrolysis – but it does so by describing a specific example, that of lead bromide, and by describing the apparatus used. We can say that the descriptions of the specific process, and of the apparatus, are *embedded* in the explanation of the general process. Thus the tasks for pupils to learn from this text are:

*1.* to identify and follow the *specific process*;
*2.* to understand the *structure* of the apparatus and the way in which the parts function as *instruments* of the process;
*3.* to reflect upon how this information explains the *general process*.

The analysis activity used with this text was designed to help pupils to tackle the text one step at a time. The instructions to pupils in pairs or threes were:

Using different coloured pens:
    First, underline all references to lead bromide and to what it becomes.
    Second, in the second paragraph underline all references to (a) the *parts* of the apparatus and (b) the *purpose* of these parts.
    Third, working on the enlarged figure, label the parts and explain what they do.
    Fourth, mark and number in the text each separate step in the process of electrolysis.
    Optional, construct a flow diagram showing the process of electrolysis.

An example of the marked-up text of two pupils working together is presented below. What is not revealed in the marked text is the categorisation of information by colour. However, the annotated diagram with notes for a flow diagram which follow does provide evidence of an intelligent analysis of the information. This is the basic objective of this type of exercise.

**What happens during electrolysis?**

If we now consider the electrolysis of lead bromide we may be able to work out the sequence of events which ends with the production of lead and bromine.

We know that lead bromide is an ionic compound and that the solid form consists of a giant structure of lead and bromide ions. When we heat the solid it fuses (melts) and the strong bonds holding the ions in the crystal lattice are broken (Kinetic Theory, Section 1.3). Molten lead bromide is made up of lead ions, $Pb^{2+}$ and bromide ions, $Br^-$ all moving in a random fashion. Putting a pair of electrodes into the melt, however, seems to direct the movement of the ions. The electrodes are connected to a battery or other source of direct current and so electrons are being 'pumped' from the negative pole of the battery to the cathode. Because the electron flow enters the electrolyte at the cathode, it is negatively charged and another way of defining a cathode is to say that it is the electrode by which electrons enters an apparatus from an external circuit. The electrons cannot 'jump' across from the cathode to the anode and yet they must be continually leaving the cathode and arriving at the anode in order to return to the battery and complete the circuit. How are the moving ions connected with this electron flow? Why should the lead ions, $Pb^{2+}$, and the bromide ions, $Br^-$, move towards the electrodes? Are they attracted to one electrode only or both?

We can answer all these questions by saying simply that 'opposite charges attract'. When the current is switched on and the electrons flow along the wire to the cathode, making it negatively charged, the positively charged lead ions are attracted to it and the negatively charged bromide ions are attracted to the positively charged anode. As each bromide ion reaches the anode it gives up an electron and becomes once again an atom of bromine:

$$Br^- \rightarrow Br + e^-$$

(Remember that bromide ions are formed when each bromine atom gains an electron; consequently when a bromide ion loses an electron to the anode it must become a bromine atom again.)

The bromine atoms join in pairs to form bromine molecules:

$$Br \rightarrow Br_2(g)$$

and so bromine vapour is evolved.

The electron removed from the bromine ion is passed on through the carbon electrode and the copper connecting wire to the battery; thus the current is kept flowing.

5

*5 (i)*

At the cathode each lead ion receives two electrons from those flowing from the battery, through the connecting wire and the carbon rod, and so becomes a lead atom:

*5 (ii)*

$$Pb^{2+} + 2^{e-} \rightarrow \bar{P}b(1)$$

The lead atoms bond together to form the giant structure of metallic lead.

During electrolysis, therefore, the ions are discharged and this giving of electrons to the ions by the cathode, and taking of electrons from the negatively charged ions by the anode, keeps the current flowing in the circuit. Within the electrolyte, however, the electrons are not handed on like buckets of water in a chain, as they are in metals, but are carried by the ions, which can be compared to one group of individuals taking full buckets of water from the tap to the fire and others taking empty ones back from the fire to the taps (13.3).

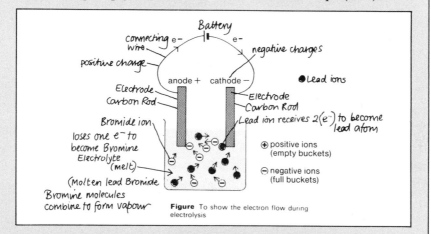

**Figure** To show the electron flow during electrolysis

The ions which carry positive charges and which are therefore attracted to the cathode are called cations. Metal ions and hydrogen ions are cations. Anions are those ions carrying negative charges and are attracted to the anode: these are the ions of non-metals and of radicals such as sulphate, nitrate and carbonate.

From L. Davies, M. J. Denial, A. W. Locke and M. E. Reay, *Investigating Chemistry*

**Notes for a flow diagram**

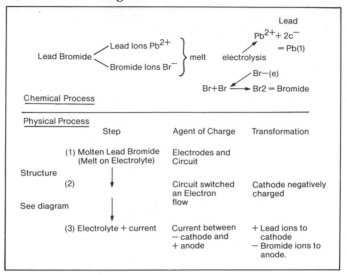

## Analysis activities: summary

In addition to the examples introduced in earlier chapters, two examples of analysis activities have been presented in this chapter: underlining and labelling.

The way in which these analysis activities may be combined with reconstruction activities like table and diagram completion in multi-darts has also been illustrated. Further examples of analysis activities are given in Chapter 5 and in *Learning from the Written Word*.

Notes on the potential of each activity and practical considerations to be borne in mind are given below.

## 1. Text marking: underlining, labelling and segmenting

### Potential

*1.* Text marking enables pupils physically to 'pin down' important parts of the text.

*2.* Even the simplest underlining involves classification of some kind, eg sorting out cause and effect.

*3.* Text marking is an 'active' learning activity.

*4.* It provides teachers with clear insights into pupils' thinking.

*5.* In labelling activities particularly, pupils are led to ask questions about the text and often go beyond their original brief.

*6.* Text marking is useful for picking out ideas 'buried' or hidden in the text.

7. Transfer to private study is likely.

8. Text marking is an ideal starting point for tabular or diagrammatic representation.

9. It may be used with any type of text.

10. It directs attention first to information constituents and then to information structure.

11. It allows information structure to be used as a framework for learning.

**Considerations**

1. Selecting information targets requires prior analysis of the text by the teacher.

2. Decisions about the number of labels, refinement of labelling, and when to provide them are determined in part by text structure and knowledge of pupils, but also by pupil response in the actual text-based lesson.

3. Too many targets or labels are confusing for pupils. (We suggest starting with no more than five.)

4. On the other hand, once pupils start work, they may find that they require a more refined categorisation – so they and/or the teacher can then extend the number of labels.

5. Frequently categories are not mutually exclusive. Pupils can be told this before or after they have started working on the text.

6. Discoveries of the kind described above frequently provide the stimulus for discussion about content and classification.

## 2. Table and diagram construction

**Potential**

1. Table and diagram construction involve the most sophisticated analysis of the text.

2. They are desirable, probably essential, for examination pupils.

3. They bring out aspects of text and relations often not apparent in any other reading of text.

4. They result in powerful summaries for revision purposes.

5. They may be done as a whole class activity, as a group activity, or by (experienced) individual pupils for homework.

6. They can be used as source material for a written summary or essay.

**Considerations**

1. It is essential for pupils to have prior experience of *completion* of tables and diagrams.

2. They should be preceded by underlining and labelling of information in the text.

3. They require that teacher and perhaps pupils are sensitive to text types and to possible representations for text types, eg flow diagram for process, hierarchies for classification, etc, as outlined in the notes on table and diagram completion.

## 3. Pupil-generated questions

**Potential**

*1.* Pupils have the opportunity to ask about what they don't know.
*2.* They can identify parts of the text which are confusing.
*3.* They can search the text for answers, or seek beyond it.
*4.* Motivation is provided.
*5.* Dimensions of content are brought out in the process.
*6.* This is a useful approach when text is limited or ambiguous.
*7.* It may be a starting point for a topic or project.

**Considerations**

*1.* A decision has to be made about which part of text to present: the beginning, so that pupils can go forward into it; the middle, so that they can go backwards and forwards; the end, so that they can work backwards.
*2.* Pupil-generated questions usually require supporting resources because many pupils will want to go beyond the immediate text.

## 4. Multi-darts

**Potential**

*1.* These are more or less obligatory when pupils are working on longer complex stretches of text.
*2.* They enable pupils to deal with different frames in different ways.
*3.* They provide practice in varying the style and pace of reading according to the reader's purpose and the nature of the text.
*4.* They give pupils as well as teachers the opportunity to evaluate the effectiveness of particular darts for particular purposes.

**Considerations**

As for each separate activity.

## Reading activities: summary

In this chapter, the potential of both reconstruction and analysis activities has been illustrated with examples, and summarised. A tabular summary of the total set of examples examined to this point, and in Chapter 4 and Chapter 5, is presented in Table 5.

*Table 5*

| Text | Text type | Reading activity | Page |
|------|-----------|------------------|------|
| Tooth structure | Structure | Labelling, underlining, table construction | 17, 80 |
| Static electricity | Instruction | Underlining | 25 |
| Expansion | Concept-principle | Deletion | 51 |
| The eye | Structure | Deletion, diagram completion | 54 |
| Volume/Plasticine | Instruction/process | Sequencing | 58 |
| Gravity | Concept | Underlining | 63 |
| Electrolysis | Structure/process | Underlining, diagram labelling, flow-chart construction | 65–70 |
| Bunsen burner | Instruction | Sequencing | 90 |
| Solids, liquids, gases | Classification | Table construction, underlining, labelling | 94–96 |
| Roots | Structure | Diagram labelling, table completion | 99 |
| Barometer | Mechanism | Diagram labelling and annotation, text underlining | 103–105 |
| Sedimentary rocks | Process | Underlining, labelling and table construction | 109–112 |
| Electric current | Concept-principle | Segmenting, labelling | 113–116 |
| Spallanzani | Theory | Segmenting, labelling | 117–120 |
| Respiration | Multiple frame: process, classification, concept-principle | Labelling table construction | 122–128 |

The extent to which the selection and design of an appropriate reading activity is determined by the teacher's understanding of text structure has been emphasised throughout this and earlier chapters. It is with a more detailed exploration of the notion of text structure that the next chapter is concerned.

# 4
# Towards a Description of Variation in Science Texts

How are the differences amongst science texts to be identified, especially those differences relating to information constituents and structure?

We approach this question by taking a closer look at how the reading activities outlined in Chapter 3 were designed.

**In all of the reading activities to date, attention has been directed to important constituents of information.**

The particular information constituents in each case varied, as did the reading activity.

In the first example, on the 'Expansion of Materials', attention was directed to *instances* or *examples* of expansion and contraction as applied in engineering design. The method used to focus attention was indirect: specific words were deleted.

In the second, attention was directed to the *parts* of the eye and their *function*. The method used was again indirect: both words and diagram labels were deleted. In the third example, attention was directed to the *steps* in an experiment and to a consideration of the ordering of those steps. Each step was presented as a separate segment of text. Pupils had to make decisions about the order of steps. In the fourth example, on 'Gravity', a much more direct instruction was used to get pupils to focus on those parts of the passage which referred to *definitions* and *principles* of gravity. In the fifth example, the important elements of content were again made the focus of attention by the direct instructions to find the *materials* undergoing change in a process, to find the *parts* of the structure which effected these changes, and to find the *steps* in a process.

In sum, in these exercises, pupils were encouraged to reflect upon examples of applications of a principle, or the parts of a structure and their function, or the steps in a procedure, or definitions or principles of a concept, or the materials, instruments and steps of a process.

The focus of the study was varied as a function of the information constituents seen to be important.

How were these information constituents identified?

A first answer might be to say that they were there – present in the text. In fact, this would not be strictly true. It is not examples, or steps, or definitions, or parts of a structure which are in a text, but certain *words*, *phrases*, or *sentences* which represent these realities.

We might say that we find the realities or information constituents 'behind' the text, by sifting through and sorting the words and sentences which represent them. For example, in the conservation experiment, it is the sequence of active imperative verbs: 'collect', 'make', 'fill', 'slide', 'read off', which signal to us that steps are to be followed. But we cannot make use of these signals and label them 'steps' without bringing our own experience and knowledge to bear on the task.

**Implicit knowledge of both language and the real world is used to make judgements about information constituents.**

This implicit knowledge is also used to make judgements about information structure.

## Information structure

We have shown how science texts vary with respect to just one or two elements of content. We want now to show how they consistently vary according to *information structure.*

The fact that a number of texts vary with respect to one information constituent is not, in itself, an indication that they vary with respect to structure.

**We proposed earlier that information structures could be differentiated if, as a primary condition, they consisted of certain constituents which consistently go together, or cohere, as actors, settings and events do in a story structure.**

We will now examine, in detail, the examples of text we have been using to see if each consists of elements which go together in this way. The method we will use will be to label segments of each text with respect to their information constituents, or slots. We will then *list*, for each text, the slots which have been identified. We will begin here by examining three of the extracts used in Chapter 3.

| Information constituents of extract | Information constituents of extract | Information constituents of extract |
|---|---|---|
| *Volume experiment* (page 58) | *Gravity text* (page 63) | *The eye* (page 54) |
| steps | definitions | parts of structure |
| materials | restrictions on | location of parts |
| apparatus | definitions | properties of parts |
| conditons/cautions | principles | function of parts |
| results/ | instances/examples | |
| outcome | measures of | |
| | concept-principle | |

What differences amongst the texts are indicated by the listings of their information constituents?

First, what is present in one text is not found in the others; the clustering of information constituents in each text varies. Each example is representative of a type of text, so we can say that the elements are more or less exclusive to that text type. However, there are some exceptions to this rule, and this is a point to which we return later.

Second, the information constituents go together in a way that is not accidental. We can say that they are more or less interdependent. Furthermore, this going together of elements reflects the way things are interdependent in the real world.

*Experiments* and practical acitivites, for instance, cannot be undertaken without *steps*, and without *materials*; and *apparatus*, whether in the form of a beaker or a cooking bowl, is also required.

In real life, when a *concept* or *principle* is introduced, or even before it is, *instances, measures, examples*, are provided.

Similarly, a *physical structure*, whether it is the structure of a tooth or a bridge, is by definition not a structure without its *parts*, their *location* and *function*. So we can say that there are certain obligatory relations amongst the information constituents of a structure which always hold.

The third way in which the texts are differentiated is through the language units which represent constituents.

**In different texts the information constituents are represented by language units that differ in size and in arrangement.**

In texts describing a structure, for instance, the different information constituents are represented in very small chunks of text, but these chunks are more or less the same size and they appear at regular intervals. This is not true of the chunks of information in concept-principle texts which are varied in size, and for which there are a number of optional arrangements. This variation in the size and distribution of language units has immediate implications for the reading of different texts. Some require frequent short breaks for reflection while others demand a searching and sifting of the text for critical elements. This was reflected in the reading activities designed for each text.

In sum, the texts used in science may be distinguished by reference to three criteria:

*1.* the presence or absence of certain information constituents (or slots);
*2.* the existence of certain relations amongst these constituents:
*3.* the size and distribution of the language units in the text which represent the different constituents.

Through reference to these criteria, three distinct information structures have been identified. We can now label each text according to its structure. The labels which have been chosen are intended to provide an indication of the general topic of the structure.

The text which gives instructions to experiment is labelled an *instruction* text.

The text which introduces the concept of gravity is labelled a *concept-principle* text.

The one which describes the structure of the tooth is classified as a *structure* text.

These three structures do not constitute the total set of structures which we have identified, but they are representative of structures which occur in instructional and expository texts in science and geography in particular.

**The examples provide evidence that science texts do vary according to information structure or frame.**

The method for identifying the structure of texts was not developed in a vacuum. Our approach to text variation in science has been informed by recent work in linguistics and cognitive psychology, but it has been more directly shaped by collaboration with the science teachers involved in the project.

The starting point was our joint effort to select reading activities appropriate for a class, context, and text. The outcome has been a 'sorting' of several hundred examples of science texts into 'like' types. The basis for classifying these types and the labels for them derived from the pooled judgement of the project team, of science teachers, and research associates.

The question is, what is it that gives rise to the structures which have been identified, and how can knowledge of structure enable us to direct our pupils' learning from text?

## Text structure as a function of topic type

Our hypothesis about text structure is very simple. It is this: while it is possible to envisage an infinite number of *topics* which might be written about in the sciences and humanities, there is a strictly limited set of *topic types*.

A *topic type* represents a class of topics which share the same information constituents or slots. For instance, we have shown how two distinct topics – a suspension bridge and tooth structure – share the same information constituents: 'parts', 'location of parts', 'properties of parts', and 'function of parts'. Where these constituents occur in a text, the text belongs to the topic type *physical structure*. In the same way, texts which describe different processes (and hence which have different topics) like electroloysis, the formation of sedimentary rock, and paper-making, all belong to the same topic type: *process*. Despite their different topics the information in the texts can be classified according to the same categories: 'state or form of object/material', 'location', 'instrument or agent of change', 'action', 'step or stage of process'.

The very consistent structuring of information in the way described is not, we suggest, accidental. It arises from the fact that objects and events in real life, especially in science, are structured in quite consistent ways. It follows that in the texts which describe certain objects and events in science, that structure is reflected. We can say that when one is writing about certain kinds of things in science, the writing is constrained by the nature of the thing being written about.

This is the kind of knowledge which is used implicitly, and usually unconsciously, by writers of text books. It is the kind of knowledge which is also used implicitly and unconsciously by readers who are successful in learning from text.

**This is why we propose that explicit knowledge of structure will, in the first instance, enable teachers to direct their pupils to regular patterns of information. It will subsequently enable the pupils to learn to do this consciously. Knowledge of structure provides a framework for reading and learning, and a framework for writing and notemaking.**

**Our long term aim is to help pupils to acquire the specific frames – the information structures – required for interpreting and writing texts in science.**

We know very little about the frames possessed by our pupils. There is evidence that implicit knowledge of the *story* frame is acquired very early by young children through experience of stories. It seems likely, too, that early and continuing experience of instructions may enable pupils to identify and use an *instruction* frame with confidence from the earliest days of schooling.

The question is, how are the frames required for interpreting different science texts to be acquired by our pupils, and how can we provide support for pupils in dealing with the different information structures they will encounter?

A first step is the identification of at least the principal information structures of science texts.

A second is to show how reading demands vary with the different information structures.

A third is to show how carefully designed reading activities can help pupils meet the demands of text variations.

These are the issues we now take up.

**A limited set of topic types giving rise to distinct information structures or frames**

We have proposed that there is a finite set of topic types which occur in science. These topic types are defined by their information constituents and hence represent certain information structures or frames.

**In this book we deal with seven topic types which consistently occur in science and some humanities text books.**

We do not claim that this set is exhaustive nor that our descriptions of the text types is definitive; nor indeed, as we have tried to show elsewhere, is it exclusive to science (*Learning from the Written Word*).

## The system of classification

What are science texts about? Science texts used in school deal with three broad categories of things:

*Activities*: experimenting, observing, and learning how to learn from doing.

*Phenomena*: like plants and animals, rocks and materials, or structures, mechanisms and processes of one kind or another.

*Ideas*: about concepts and principles of laws, and about theories and tests of theories.

These things we suggest are the realities behind science. They are the distinct *activities* writers want pupils to engage in, the *phenomena* they want them to observe, the *ideas* they want them to embrace and develop.

We propose, therefore, that science texts may be classified into three broad categories, according to what they are about: activities, phenomena and ideas. Within each of these categories it is possible to identify further distinct types of text, differentiated more specifically according to topic types or information structure. In Table 7, we list seven text types and define them with reference to two criteria:

the sort of thing they are about – the topic type;

the information constituents which we expect to find in them.

The topic type of the text gives us the *frame* or *structure label* – for instance, 'instruction', 'mechanism', and so on. The information constituents which make up the structure of the frame we can think of as the *slots* of the frame.

The use of the notion of slots highlights the fact that frames are abstract entities – the 'ideal' paradigms against which we can check any given text. In some texts all of the slots of a given frame may be filled. In other texts some slots may be empty.

The usefulness of the notion of slots is apparent when we come to analyse a text in practice, because we can construct a table for each frame with columns for the slots and then physically fill in the slots with the appropriate references from the text. This is the method we will use to illustrate the different text types from now on, and which we show with an analysis for the 'Tooth structure' text presented in the Introduction (page 17).

*Table 6  Physical structure text – tooth structure*

| Name of structure or part | Location | Property | Function |
|---|---|---|---|
| A tooth (has) the crown | projecting above the gum | | |
| the neck | embedded in the soft gum | | |
| the root | out of sight | | anchoring the tooth in the bony socket |
| the dentine | inside the tooth | a fairly hard material which contains some living cells | |
| the dentine | | cannot withstand wear | |
| the dentine | in crown and neck | is covered with a layer of *enamel* | |
| the dentine | in the root | covered with a substance called | |
| cement socket | | *cement* | helps fix the tooth in its *socket* |
| the pulp cavity: nerves small artery small vein | inside the dentine in centre of the tooth | is hollow containing *nerves*, a *small artery*, a *small vein* | |

Table 7 *Text types differentiated according to frames*

| | Frame/label | Slots/Information Constituents | | | | | |
|---|---|---|---|---|---|---|---|
| **Activities** | Instruction or recipe | action step/ procedure | material | apparatus | caution or condition | result | interpretation |
| **Phenomena** | Classification or Categorisation | example/ group | property/ feature | comparison | test of property feature | system/ dimensions of classification | |
| | Structure | name of structure or *part* (+ – substance) | location | property | function | | |
| | Mechanism | name of mechanism or *part* (+ – substance) | action | function | location | property | object/ phenomenon acted upon |
| | Process | time or stage | state or form of phenomen- on | agent instrument of change | location | property or structure | transformation action/ reaction |
| | Concept-principle | definition | law or principle | restrictions | application instances examples | analogy | measure |
| | Hypothesis-theory | hypothesis question problem | context of | tests of hypothesis (method) | results evidence | interpret- ations | hypotheses |

## Analysis of text frames

What are the rules we follow in identifying the information structure or frame of a text?

First, we start by making a prediction about the frame label. This is based on a judgement about the topic type.

Second, we test the prediction by filling in the appropriate frame table.

*1.* What is filled in any given slot must actually be present in the text: ie, only what is explicitly given in the text goes in.
*2.* Anything which does not clearly fit into any slot must be left out. What is left out of the frame table we call 'text residue'.

We have already pointed out that the slots of a frame are not always filled by the natural texts of our sample; we have found that in school texts certain slots are often left empty in order to reduce the information load. In other cases slots may be left empty because too much has been assumed by the writer or because the writer has chosen to reduce the information load.

**Identifying gaps in slots, or empty slots, is as important a part of the analysis as is filling slots with references which fit.**

The test of whether a frame fits a text is not emptiness of slots, but 'text residue'.

*If there is substantial text residue, it is an indication that the wrong frame may have been predicted.* Alternatively, there may be more than one frame structuring the text (as in the 'Electrolysis' text in Chapter 3) or finally there may be 'intrusions'. The judgement is made after the analysis.

The slots and their labels are not rigorously defined. This is quite deliberate. They are intended to be useful. The labels are general descriptions intended to be comprehensible to the non-specialist. In some cases there are either/or labels for slots, like 'caution or condition' in the instruction frame. The analysis is intended to provide information useful in designing a reading activity.

Slots are not always mutually exclusive. In the 'Tooth structure' text, for example, it is a *property* of the tooth that it is hollow, containing nerves, a small artery, and a small vein; but the nerves, artery and vein are also *parts* of the tooth. In a rigorous linguistic analysis it would be appropriate to write in a rule which would tell us into exactly which slot these references would go. We do not think that such precision is appropriate for our present purposes.

Finally, the length of the stretch of the text which fits a single frame varies considerably. When the frame is a physical structure the stretch of text which fits this frame is usually quite short, from two to five paragraphs;

the stretch of text which follows may be a description of a process or a principle. In contrast, a text describing a theory may run to several pages. Furthermore, it may have embedded in it a description of a physical structure, as we saw in the electrolysis text, or an introduction to a concept.

## Ordering and embedding of structures

Thus, it is important to think of *the frames as being units of information* which are *represented in units of written language of different sizes*; and to think of *continuous text as being patterned or structured by the ordering and embedding of units.* The examples of texts which have been used to illustrate variation in structure are, on the surface, relatively straightforward passages.

We might ask, is it always easy to identify the structure of a text? The answer is, first, that it is easier to do so with models or paradigms of different text structures as a starting point, and secondly that it does depend on the text. Also, it is easier to identify the structure when a text is organised by a single structure than when there is ordering and embedding of structures.

Finally, we can say that when the structure of a text is more or less 'tidy', as in the case of the initial examples, it is not difficult to identify the structure.

**However, not all the passages of continuous prose that we want to use in school are organised by a single structure; and many of the texts we have available are 'untidy'. For this reason we think it will be useful to look at examples of text which do not fit our paradigms so neatly.**

We will re-examine two examples of texts in which different structures are embedded; and one which we think is 'untidy' in its structuring. It is worth noting that the examples are all relatively short and simple, so structuring is not necessarily more consistent over short simple stretches of prose than it is over larger chunks, like chapters. On the other hand, we do expect to find more structures and greater embedding of different structures over longer, more complex, passages.

The first example we will examine is the first extract for which a reading activity was prepared (see page 51): 'Expansion', reprinted in its original form below.

> *1.* Materials expand when they are heated. Most materials expand, or become larger, when they are heated, and contract, or become smaller, when they are cooled. The expansion of solid materials, like iron

and brass, is so small that it is not noticed unless special apparatus is used to measure it and to show that it is, in fact, occurring.

*2.* The expansion of solids. Push the metal ball of a ball and ring apparatus through the ring. Heat the ball and, when it is red hot, lift it with tongs and place it on the ring. The ball does not fall through the ring. It has expanded. What happens when the ball cools and contracts?

*3.* Heat the bar of a bar and gauge apparatus. Try to push the bar into the gauge. It does not fit. Allow the bar to cool. It now fits into the gauge for it has contracted in length.

*4.* Lay a thick iron rod across two bricks. Use Plasticine to attach a straw to one end of a knitting needle. Place the needle, so that the straw is upright, on one of the bricks and underneath the rod. Then heat the rod. The straw turns. Why? Now allow the rod to cool. The straw now turns in the opposite direction. Why?

*5.* Expansion and contraction can be a nuisance or even cause damage. Therefore, engineers make allowance for expansion and contraction. Steam pipes are built with loops, bends and moveable collars so that no damage is done when the pipes become hot and expand. Telephone wires and power cables are left slack so they do not snap when they contract in cold weather. Large metal bridges rest loosely on rollers or plastic pads built into their supports.

*6.* Then expansion can take place freely and no damage is done to the bridges. Narrow tar-filled gaps are sometimes made in concrete roads so that cracking does not occur when the concrete expands. The rails on a railway track are welded together to make a single rail that is often more than one kilometre in length. This rail is heated and stretched. It is then fixed down firmly in the expanded state so that it contracts only slightly when the weather becomes colder. The pendulums of clocks are sometimes provided with wooden or plastic bobs and adjustable nuts. Wood and plastic do not expand as much as metals. The nut of a pendulum is turned so that the position of the bob is altered and allowance made for expansion and contraction.

From C. Windridge, *General Science*, Book 1.

In the reading activity for the above extract, attention was indirectly focused on examples of the application of a principle. So we might expect that the structure of the passage would be labelled concept-principle. In practice we do find, in paragraph 1, references to the information structures of concept-principle: a statement of a principle — 'Metals expand when they are heated' — and also references to *measures* of expansion. In paragraphs 5 and 6, *examples* and *illustrations* of the principle and *application* of it are presented.

But what is happening in paragraphs 2, 3 and 4?

The reader is not so much required to reflect upon the principle as to test it practically. *Instructions* for testing the principle are set out in the form of references to steps, materials, apparatus, results/outcomes and even interpretation of results: 'The straw turns. Why?'

Paragraph 2, 3 and 4 are distinct from paragraphs 1, 5 and 6. Their purpose is different and the structuring of information is different. In this example an instruction frame is inserted into or embedded in the concept-principle frame; but we have little difficulty in identifying the two structures. We know from classroom experience that a quite different response is required from pupils when they reach each of these two sections of the text.

The second example of embedding of frames is to be found in the 'Electrolysis' text given on page 65. Here the embedding is more complex than in the 'Expansion' passage. The different information structures, process (a and b) and structure, are not so clearly separable. This is not surprising because the information about the 'structure' of the apparatus is serving, in this text, as a description of the 'instrument' which causes the change. Thus, in a text which is structured overall by a process frame, a 'physical structure' is so deeply embedded that in itself, it fills the '*instrument*' slot of the process frame.

Texts in which different frames are deeply embedded are very demanding. They require of the learner, in effect, a peeling-off of layers. Pupils need to be supported in this process by guidance from a teacher who knows the demands of the text.

**The notion of structure helps to explain why different sections of text and different types of text make different reading demands.**

Furthermore, a recognition of embedded structures will enable us to plan quite different reading strategies for different sections of the text. This would not be the outcome of an analysis of 'terminology' or readability level.

### Texts in which structure is violated

Our example of what we call an 'untidy' text is, on the surface, a simple set of instructions. We have underlined and labelled those parts of the text which belong to a simple instruction frame. We have put brackets around those parts of the text we found it difficult to classify.

*Experiment*

       *Step*  ,  *Material*  ,  *Apparatus*

1. <u>Look at/some pond water/under the microscope.</u>

       *Results / Outcomes*

2. <u>Can you see some living organisms in it?</u>

3. (Your teacher will now bubble some chlorine into it.)

       *Results / Outcomes*

4. <u>What do you see when you examine the chlorinated water under the microscope?</u>

5. (Try to find out where your house water supply comes from and what is done to purify it.

6. If possible visit the water works and see for yourself.)

From A. J. Mee, P. Boyd and D. Ritchie,
*Science for the Seventies*, Book 1.

What is it about the bracketed instructions that makes them difficult to classify? On the surface, the parts of the text within the brackets can be classified loosely according to our instruction categories: 'steps', 'materials', 'apparatus', and so on. But at a deeper level, they seem to violate certain *implicit rules*. The conventional instruction is implicitly addressed to 'you', the reader, as experimenter or craftsperson. When a text describes what someone else has done or will do it is (usually) not an instruction text – especially, as in this case, where the text, in the role of teacher, describes what the 'real' teacher will do. For better or for worse, our expectations of the instruction frame are not met.

The second implicit rule which is broken concerns the task(s). Conventional instructions refer to a single sequential task in a prescribed context over a specific, though implied, period of time. In this text, however, there is more than one task, and the tasks vary in magnitude and complexity from the explicit, but very limited, task of using the microscope to examine the organisms in pond water, to two complete projects for which no steps, materials or apparatus are specified. The periods of time vary too, from the limited period of present time to unspecified future times.

**When a text violates conventional structure in such ways the text is not easy to classify. Nor, we suggest, is it easy to comprehend.**

Comprehension is made possible by structuring – by the presence of a consistent frame of reference for interpreting individual facts. When the frame changes rapidly or is inconsistent, it is not easy to organise individual facts – nor, as in the case of this text, to follow different instructions.

It is not our intention here to question the effectiveness of telling pupils what their teacher will (it is hoped) do next, nor to challenge the value of visits to water works. What we do wish to draw attention to is the fact that texts which do not conform to conventional structures are not easy to comprehend. Identifying the frame of such texts is difficult and may be impossible; this poses problems for pupils as much as for teachers.

**For this reason we think it is as important to be able to recognise poorly structured texts as it is to be able to identify clearly structured examples.**

We are also concerned to show that the comprehensibility of a text is not necessarily a function of the length or complexity of words or sentences as measured by readability formulae. The way in which ideas are structured, we propose, is as significant as the words and sentences which represent them.

This is why we have chosen to draw attention to one example of a poorly structured text which is representative of many which teachers and pupils have to deal with daily.

The inconsistencies in the structuring of information in this extract are characteristic not of the complete text book from which it came, but of isolated passages in almost every text book. It is quite possible that such inconsistencies do not reflect any lack of writing expertise on the part of the authors, but rather reflect the response of these authors to a limited set of notions about what constitutes a good text book. Foremost among these are the notions that:

*1.* the language of the text (words and sentences) should be *simple* and short;
*2.* the text should be substantially supported by graphically represented information and illustrations;
*3.* the information load in the text should be kept to a minimum;
*4.* the relevance of science in real life should be made explicit.

We could not in principle challenge these objectives, but we propose that an even more important criterion for the text book is that the text itself is structured. We anticipate, furthermore, that coherent structure will at times not be achieved without a certain loss in the simplicity of the language, and a certain increase in information load.

We have proposed that even implicit knowledge of structure facilitates comprehension and learning. We have argued that explicit knowledge of structure will facilitate teaching and learning. But knowledge of structure is not usable if the structuring of the information in the text itself is not accessible.

## Summary

In this chapter we have focused on variation in science texts. We have proposed that distinct text types may be identified through reference to underlying meaning or information structure. Three broad categories of text have been identified: those dealing with *activities, phenomena* and *ideas*. Within these categories seven types of text representing distinct information structures have been proposed: *instruction, classification, structure, mechanism, process, concept-principle, hypothesis-theory*. A method for identifying the text types through reference to information structure has been outlined, and we have shown how information structure is determined by the presence or absence of certain information constituents or slots. It has also been shown that information structure determines the size and distribution of the language items of a text, and consequently determines the reading demands of different texts.

The method of analysis we have adopted here is one which enables us to distinguish amongst texts with respect to the frames which structure them. It also provides a means of identifying 'mixed' structures and of recognising lack of structure. While it has been emphasised that the analytic method is not as rigorous as would be required in a research investigation, it is, on the other hand, a more detailed method of analysis than most teachers have time for.[1]

It is not our intention, therefore, to suggest that teachers or pupils analyse texts in the way we have described, though we anticipate that will be done by some teachers. Rather, we believe that teachers who study the method and examples will then be able to use the broad parameters of the system 'on their feet', so to speak. We have argued throughout this book that sound direction of pupil reading is based on *informed analysis of text* by teachers. This we now illustrate through the presentation of examples.

### Note

1 More rigorous and refined methods of testing and validating frames are referred to in the Annotated Bibliography – Theoretical Background, pages 134–139.

# 5
# Examples of Text Types and Reading Activities in Science

In the following pages one example of each type of text is presented. The format for the analysis of each passage is consistent. It begins with a listing of the *slots of the frame* and a brief comment on the references which fill the slots of the frame.

One example of the *text type* is then presented.

This is followed by a *tabular representation* of the references categorised according to the slots of the frame.

Notes on the *reading demand* of the text type and on a typical *reading activity* for the text type follow.

Two things should be said about the examples which have been used. First, they are all extracts from text books or worksheets which have been, or are currently, in use by teachers involved in the project. With a few exceptions they have also been used with pupils. They are not artificial examples, occurring outside the classroom, but the everyday data with which we have worked. They are, however, unrepresentative in one respect – they are, for the most part, quite short. As short extracts they therefore tend to be structured by a single frame. A more complex extract which illustrates both the integration of two or more frames in a single text and a shift of frame in a single extract is presented at the end of the section.

Second, since Chapter 5 is intended to be a free-standing unit, it includes descriptions of the three types which have already been examined in some depth: instruction, structure and concept-principle.

The order in which text types are introduced corresponds approximately to the relative (structural) complexity of the frames.

## Instruction texts

We start with texts designed to give instructions: undertaking an experiment, making something, using apparatus.

In the ideal frame for instruction texts there are slots for:

*actions*, or steps, or procedures (including directions to observe or to calculate)
*materials*
*apparatus*
*cautions* or *conditions*
*results*, or *effects*, or *outcomes of procedures*
*interpretation of results.*

You will remember that in theory these slots are 'filled' by sets of references which fit into one or other slot. In practice, some slots are left empty in certain texts or are only partially filled. In the example below there are references to *steps*, to *materials* and *apparatus*, and to *results*, but the *caution* and *interpretation* slots are more or less empty, as is shown in Table 8. (In this text numbers indicate scrambled order. Identification of segments by numbers is to facilitate class discussion.)

---

**The scrambled text**
**To measure the heat given out per second by a bunsen burner flame**

  8. measure the mass of a clean dry 250 cm³ beaker
 12. add approx 50 cm³ cold water to the beaker
  3. measure the mass of the beaker plus water
 16. take the initial temperature of the water
  7. place the beaker on a tripod with a gauze
  1. set the bunsen burner onto a blue flame
 11. place the bunsen burner under the beaker
  5. start the stop-watch
 14. after about 5 minutes, remove the bunsen from under the beaker
 10. stop the stop-watch and note the reading
  2. record the new temperature of the water
 15. calculate the mass of water in the beaker (in kg)
  4. calculate the temperature rise of the water
  6. calculate the number of joules of heat received by the water, assuming that the specific heat capacity of water is 4200 J/KgK
  9. calculate the number of seconds for which the water was heated
 13. calculate the number of joules received by the water each second

From a text written by a physics teacher,
Huntingdon, Cambridgeshire

### Reading demands of instruction texts

Instruction texts may be read receptively; but this will not be a very useful strategy. The demand made by an instruction text is that the reader constructs, in his or her imagination, what should happen in reality – a sequence of steps and precautions. Reading an instruction text requires reference to reality as well as to the text. *Ideally, it involves reflection on the purpose of the activity and on outcomes.*

### Reading activities for instruction texts

Directed-reading activities for instruction texts are designed to get pupils to:

> reflect on proper *procedures* and use of *apparatus*;
> predict or anticipate necessary *precautions*;
> reflect on *results*.

One of the most widely used reading activities for instruction texts is the *scrambled text* or *sequencing activity*.

**The task for pupils is to use logical cues to arrange the segments in the order which makes the most sense or is the most practical.**

This is the reading activity which was used by a teacher in a Cambridgeshire comprehensive school with his third-year pupils before undertaking the experiment outlined in the passage. Pupils working in pairs were given the cut-up segments.

Pupil sequencing of the· segments was followed by class discussion in which precautions were also dealt with in detail; so the 'Caution' slot in the instruction frame was filled, in this case, by teacher talk. The other two slots would be filled by class discussion and notes after the experimental work had been undertaken. The teacher's observation, shared by many other science teachers, is that the scrambled text reading activity is very useful as a means of *preparation for experimental work*. It has the effect of improving performance in the laboratory, of reducing the number of pupil questions about procedure, and of encouraging reflection.

## Classification texts

The frame for classification texts is a simple one. We expect the classification frame to tell us about what phenomena are like, what their features or

Table 8 *To measure the heat given out per second by a bunsen burner flame*

| Step/procedure/action | Material | Apparatus | Caution/condition | Result | Interpretation |
|---|---|---|---|---|---|
| *Measure* – the mass | | a clean dry 250 cm$^3$ beaker | | [*Note* mass of beaker and water] | |
| *Add* to the beaker | approx 150 cm$^3$ cold water | the beaker | | | |
| *Measure* the mass of | plus water | the beaker | | [*Note* mass of beaker and water] | |
| *Take* the initial temperature | the water | | | [*Note* the temperature] | |
| *Place* | | on a tripod with a gauze, the beaker | | | |
| *Set onto* | a blue flame | the bunsen burner | | | |
| *Place* | | under the beaker the bunsen burner | | | |
| *Start* | | the stop watch | after about 5 minutes | | |

*Table 8 (cont.)*

| Step/procedure/ action | Material | Apparatus | Caution/ condition | Result | Interpretation |
|---|---|---|---|---|---|
| *Remove* | | the bunsen burner from under the beaker | | | |
| *Stop* | | the stop watch | | [*Note* time] | |
| *Record* the temperature | of the water | | | [*Note* the new temperature] | |
| *Calculate* | | | in the beaker | the mass of water (in kg) | |
| *Calculate* | | | | the temperature rise of the water | |
| *Calculate* | | | assuming that the specific heat capacity of the water is 4200 J/KgK | the number of joules received by the water | |
| *Calculate* | | | | the number of seconds for which the water was heated | |
| *Calculate* | | | | the number of joules received by the water each second | |

properties are, and how they might be classified. The slots for the classification frame are:

> *example* or *group* of phenomena
> *features* or *properties* of phenomena
> *comparison/contrast*
> *tests* of properties or features
> *system or dimensions of classification.*

In the text below, three examples or forms of phenomena are compared and contrasted through reference to their properties.

The sets of references to the particular example under discussion – solids, liquids and gases – are quite clear; so are the references to *properties*. There is also reference to the *tests* for *properties*: "This is evident from the fact that solids are very difficult to compress."

There are, however, no explicit references to the criteria for classification of the forms, eg packing, bonding. These have to be inferred from the description of *properties*. So the *basis or system* of the *classification* slot may be regarded as empty, as is illustrated in the table following the passage.

---

**Solids, liquids and gases**

The most obvious features of the way that the particles are arranged in a substance depend on whether it is a solid, a liquid, or a gas.

The particles in a solid must be held in fixed positions, otherwise solids would not retain their shapes. Moreover, the particles in a solid must be packed very tightly together. This is evident from the fact that solids are very difficult to compress. Even at a very high pressure, the change in volume is very small indeed.

In most liquids, the particles are less tightly packed than in a solid. This is evident when a solid is melted as there is usually an increase in volume on the change from solid to liquid. However, since liquids are also difficult to compress, the particles must still be very close together. The main difference between solids and liquids is that liquids have no shape. They take the shape of the container and are free to move about and can be poured. Obviously the particles in a liquid are not fixed in any definite position. They are able to move about, rolling over each other like grains of sand.

Gases not only take the shape of the vessel which contains them but also spread out to occupy the whole vessel. This is easily seen by using a coloured gas like bromine. Our picture of a gas is one in which the particles are free to move about and there are quite large spaces between them. Increasing the pressure on a gas brings the particles closer together. If this increase in pressure is large enough then the particles become as close together as in a liquid. The gas will then change into a liquid.

Text adapted by a Derbyshire chemistry teacher from C. V. Platts, *The Structure of Substances.*

**Reading demands of classification texts**

On the surface, classification texts are 'easy' to read. The major demand they make on pupils is that of inferring the system or dimensions of classification. This is not always made explicit.

**Teachers need to provide support by showing how references to properties indicate the *dimensions* or *categories* of classification.**

The classification demands of this particular text are considerable. There are two 'observable' properties of 'gases, liquids and solids': *shape* and *movement*. There are two features of particle arrangement: *spacing* of particles and *packing*. But while the observables of shape and movement can be shown to be a function of the spacing of particles, there are no observables which are a function of packing.

Evidence for packing is derived from tests of compression or from melting. Furthermore, differences between solids, liquids and gases on the *packing* dimension are expressed in terms of a continuum rather than in discrete measures.

**Reading activities for classification texts**

Reading activities for classification texts are designed to enable pupils to:
    identify or locate *examples or groups* and their *properties* or *features*;
    work out the *system for classification*;
    categorise examples according to the system of classification.

The most useful directed-reading activity for locating information is underlining. The most obvious means of categorising the information is to label and/or to construct or complete a table.

The most demanding of the three tasks is the labelling or categorising, especially in a text like the one above where labels are not explicitly given.

*Table 9  Classification text: solids, liquids and gases*

| Example or group | Property or feature | Comparison/contrast | Test of | System or dimension of classifcation |
|---|---|---|---|---|
| A solid | particles (must) be held in fixed position | | (otherwise) would not retain their shapes | |
| A solid | particles (must) be packed very tightly together | | (this is evident from the fact) difficult to compress. (Even at high pressure) change in volume very small indeed | |
| Most liquids | particles less tightly packed | | (this is evident when a solid is melted) as there is usually an increase in volume on the change from solid to liquid | |
| Liquids | particles still very close together | also still | difficult to compress | |
| Liquids | have no shape | the main difference between solids and liquids | | |
| They (liquids) | take shape of container are free to move about can be poured | | | |
| A liquid | particles – not fixed in any definite position – are able to move about, rolling over each other like grains of sand | | obviously | |

These are usually provided by the teacher. Alternatively, pupils are led through the underlining task, for instance, to a position where they can provide their own labels. The reading activity designed for this text by a teacher in a Derbyshire comprehensive school is outlined below.

**Study guide**

*1.* First, read the whole passage with care.
*2.* With a coloured crayon, underline the parts of the passage which tell you about the movement of particles.
*3.* With a crayon of different colour, underline the parts of the passage which tell you about compressing or squashing a substance.
*4.* Use the headings, 'Solid', 'Liquid' and 'Gas' to make a table which summarises how particles move.
*5.* Use the same headings to make a table which summarises how easy it is to compress a substance.
*6.* Attach this sheet firmly in your notebook on the page opposite your answers.

This straight text activity was used with upper and lower band second year pupils. Lower band pupils found the initial underlining task difficult, but, like the upper band pupils, completed the table successfully.

A group of science teachers in Suffolk designed a similar directed-reading activity text:

*1.* it started with underlining of the properties of gases, liquids and solids;
*2.* it involved pupils in differentiating between observable properties and inferred properties (ie the particle structure);
*3.* it concluded with the completion of a table, with the headings provided by the teacher, along the lines indicated below:

*Table 10*

|  | *Observable* | | *Inferred* | | |
|  | Shape | Movement | Spacing of particles | Packing | Tests of packing |
|---|---|---|---|---|---|
| Solids Liquids Gases |  |  |  |  |  |

Pupils worked on the first section, ie up to the double line, before doing the second.

An alternative tabular summary was suggested by a member of the project team where the role of finding evidence is highlighted as:

*Table 11*

|  | Solids | Liquids | Gases |
|---|---|---|---|
| Packing; Evidence<br><br>Mobility; Evidence |  |  |  |

**Notes**

*1.* No single watertight reading activity is recommended for a text-type. We have shown a number of alternatives. On the other hand, quite specific sorts of activities are seen as appropriate for particular types of text.

All of the (science) teachers and research workers who have studied the example above have suggested some form of *tabular representation* along the lines indicated above. This is a strong indication that the nature of the text determines the type of reading activity.

*2.* The reading activities outlined above included at least two or three directed reading activities, underlining, labelling and table completion. This is typical of text-based lessons – the majority involve multiple reading activities or multi-darts.

## Structure texts

Structure texts often have the term 'structure' in the title, as in the example below from the MacKean text, *Introduction to Biology*. The frame of a structure text, as we have already seen, has slots for:

> *names* of parts;
> *properties* of parts;
> *location* of parts;
> *function* of parts.

Structure texts are usually accompanied by a diagram. If not, a diagram should be provided. In the diagram, *parts* are labelled, and their *location* is shown; but a description of the *properties* and their *function* is usually not shown in the diagram.

A close study of the text below indicates that all the slots of the structure frame are filled, and that there is a focus on *properties* and *functions* – culminating in references which serve both to describe *properties* and explain *function* in the last sentences.

It is worth noting that some of the parts of the root which are referred to in the text are not labelled in the diagram. We will make use of this in planning a reading activity.

### General structure of roots

Usually white, roots cannot develop chlorophyll. They never bear leaves or axillary buds.

### Function

Roots anchor the plant firmly in the soil and prevent its being blown over by the wind. They absorb water and mineral salts from the soil and pass them into the stem. Frequently they can act as food stores.

### Detailed structure – Epidermis

This is a layer of cells without a cuticle. The younger regions, particularly those with root hairs, permit the uptake of water and solutes.

### Cortex

The cortex consists of large, thin-walled cells with air spaces between them. The cortical cells store food material and the innermost layer of cells may regulate the inward passage of water and dissolved substances.

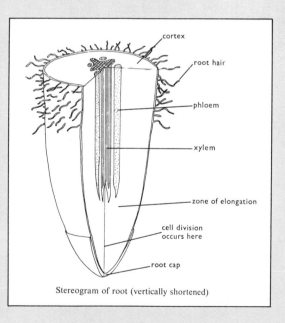

Stereogram of root (vertically shortened)

### Vascular Tissue

This is in the centre of the root, and initially the phloem strands lie between the radial arms of the central xylem. The branches that form the lateral roots grow from this region and force their way through the cortex, bursting through the outer layer to reach the soil. The centrally

*(continued on page 102)*

*Table 12 Roots structure text* (from D. G. Mackean, *Introduction to Biology*)

| Name of structure or part | Location | Property | Function |
|---|---|---|---|
| Roots<br>They | | usually white, cannot develop chlorophyll, never bear leaves or axillary buds | |
| Roots | | | anchor the plant firmly in the soil and prevent it being blown over by the wind |
| They | | absorb water and mineral salts from the soil and | pass them into the stem<br><br>frequently act as food stores |
| (Epidermis) this | | is a layer of cells without a cuticle | |
| The younger regions particularly those with root hairs | | | permit the uptake of water and solutes |
| The cortex (thin-walled cells) | | consists of large thin-walled cells with air spaces between them | |

Table 12 (cont.)

| Name of structure or part | Location | Property | Function |
|---|---|---|---|
| The cortical cells | | | store food material |
| The innermost cells | | | may regulate the inward passage of water and dissolved substances |
| (Vascular tissue) This | is in the centre of the root | | |
| The phloem strands (the central xylem) | lie between the radial axis of the central xylem | | |
| The branches that form the lateral roots | from this region/through the cortex/ to reach the soil | grow and force their way, bursting through the outer layer | |
| The vascular tissue | centrally placed | well-adapts the root to the strain that it is likely to experience along its length. This makes an interesting comparison with the cylindrical distribution of vascular tissues in the stem and the lateral strain to which it might be subjected | |

> placed vascular tissue well-adapts the root to the strain that it is likely to experience along its length. This makes an interesting comparison with the cylindrical distribution of vascular tissue in the stem and the lateral strain to which it might be subjected.
>
> From D. G. MacKean, *Introduction to Biology*. In its published form this extract is accompanied by numerous illustrations.

### Reading demands of structure texts

Structure texts cannot be read receptively. Our experience with pupils and teachers indicates that they are rejected by a majority of readers.

**Structure texts require reference to the diagram as well as to the text at short and frequent intervals.**

There are no rewards from reading structure texts, except those of learning the parts and their function.

### Reading activities for structure texts

Reading activities for structure texts are designed to get pupils:

*1.* to locate and learn the names of *parts*;
*2.* to relate the *properties* of *parts* to their *function*.

This can be done by getting pupils to break their reading of the text at very short intervals in order to work at text and diagram. The breaking of the read is achieved by deleting some of the information from either the text or the diagram. In the 'Roots' text, reference is made to some parts which are not labelled in the diagram.

The first pupil task is to use the information in the text to complete the *labelling* of the diagram. The second task is to use the information in the text to annotate the diagram by describing the properties of the parts and their functions.

The activity of diagram completion is extensively used by the science teachers with whom we have worked for the learning of structures and mechanisms.

**All are agreed that reading of the text without working at the diagram is not to be recommended.**

The potential of diagram completion as a means of learning is also highly rated; it is, however, more time-consuming than a straight read. Nevertheless, it is one reading activity which pupils can undertake for homework providing time is allowed for a feedback session as a follow-up.

## Mechanism texts

A mechanism text has basically the same frame as a structure text but it has additional slots. So we expect to find references to:

*names* of parts;
*properties* and *location* of parts;
*action* and *function* of parts;
*phenomenon acted* upon and its *properties*.

The reasons for differentiating between structure and mechanism are discussed subsequently. At this point we simply draw attention to differences between the example below, 'The aneroid barometer', which we label mechanism, and the 'Roots structure' example previously discussed. In the text below, the 'working' of the structure is as important as the parts. The structure – the barometer – acts upon air, and is acted upon by it. So there are references to the *phenomenon* acted upon and to the *action of parts* as well as to *parts*, their *location*, and *properties*, as shown in Table 13 on page 106.

---

### The aneroid barometer

Although the mercury barometer can be a comparatively accurate measuring instrument, it is rather bulky and 'spillable'.

Another instrument for measuring atmospheric pressure is the Aneroid Barometer ('aneroid' means 'without liquid'). In the aneroid barometer, air pressure is balanced against a powerful spring.

The vacuum box is made from thin corrugated metal. The two opposite sides are kept apart by the pull of the spring while air pressure tries to squash the box flat. The bottom of the box and the bottom of the spring are both fixed to a solid base-plate. Any increase in air pressure will move the top of the box and the spring downwards; any decrease in pressure will allow the spring to expand and move the top of the box upwards.

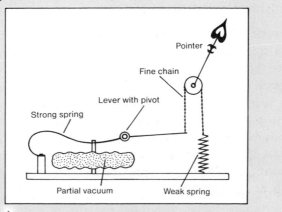

> Because the amount of movement is very small indeed, it is increased by a lever, chain and pulley system which transfers the movement to a pointer on a dial.
>
> A more sensitive instrument can be made by using vacuum boxes stacked one on top of the other. This will produce a greater movement at the top of the top box for any given change in air pressure.
>
> Although the aneroid barometer is usually less accurate than the mercury barometer, it has the great advantage of being portable and will work in any position.
>
> From L. J. Campbell and R. J. Carlton (eds), *Foundation Science*.

### Reading demands of mechanism texts

These we believe to be considerable. Mechanism texts, like structure texts, require that elements of text are accurately related to parts of the diagram. But there is a further demand: that of relating the *action of parts* to the *phenomenon* acted upon or measured. Typically, as in the case of 'The aneroid barometer', this involves taking account of the *properties* of both the *parts* of the mechanism and of the *phenomenon* acted upon or measured. In addition, *action* is often reciprocal.

**In effect, therefore, mechanism texts require of the reader the simultaneous use of both a structure frame and the process frame.**

The process frame is introduced immediately following the discussion of mechanism.

### Reading activities for mechanism texts

These are substantially the same as activities for structure texts; but they incorporate some means of drawing attention to the *phenomenon* acted upon and to the *action of parts*.

The directed reading activity below was designed for mixed-ability third and fourth years in a Derbyshire school. The teacher, who worked from the instructions to pupils, commented on the very high level of concentration of pupils working on the text and diagrams, and on successful learning outcomes. (A typical example of an annotated text is on page 105. It has not been corrected.) Pupils were provided with the diagram, Sheet 1, and the text, Sheet 2, separately.

**Sheet 1**

The lever pivot is the message amplifier.
As the vibrations come up the other half
of the lever near the strong spring (which
are only small vibrations) as it comes
up. the pivot makes the vibration bigger
moving the chain and the pointer.

This strong spring
Keeps the sides of
the box apart.
This is necessary
because if they did
meet you would get
a false reading

This is the
part of the
barometer where
there is almost
no air.

This part moves
when air
presses on it.

Pointer

Fine chain

Lever with pivot

Strong spring

Partial vacuum

Weak spring

Vaccum box
This part is affected by air pressure
changing by the air inside and
on the outside.
If it is high pressure the air
on the outside moves in which
moves the pivot.
Then this moves the chain and the
weak spring which moves the
pointer.
If it is low pressure the box
moves out because of the air
inside and this does the same
but the other way.

Table 13  *Mechanism text – the aneroid barometer*

| Mechanism of part (+– substance) | Action | Function | Location | Property | Object/ phenomenon acted upon | Residue |
|---|---|---|---|---|---|---|
| Powerful spring | is balanced against | | * in the aneroid barometer | | air pressure | |
| * the vacuum box | | are kept apart | | is made from thin corrugated metal | | |
| * the two opposite sides | | | | | | |
| the spring | by the pull of | | | | | while |
| the box | tries to squash flat | | | | * air pressure | |
| * the bottom of the box and the bottom of the spring | | | a solid base-plate | are fixed to | | both |

| Mechanism of part (+ − substance) | Action | Function | Location | Property | Object/ phenomenon acted upon | Residue |
|---|---|---|---|---|---|---|
| the top of the box and the spring | will move | | downwards | * increase in | air pressure | any |
| the spring | to expand | will allow | | * decrease in | air pressure | any |
| the top of the box | and move | | upwards | | | |
| | the amount of * movement | | | very small indeed | | because it is |
| a level chain and pulley system | transfers movement to | | | is increased by | | which |
| a pointer on a dial | | | | | | which |

* indicates starting point of statement in text

→ arrows point to next reference, so table has to be read from right to left as well as from left to right

*Text residue*: note items in 'residue' are simply logical or linguistic connectives

---

**Pupil instructions**

In order to work on the diagram on Sheet 1 you will need to check the explanation of the diagram on Sheet 2.

*1.* Find the part of the barometer where there is almost no air, and therefore *almost no air pressure.*

*2.* Shade in the empty space, or *partial vacuum*, where there is almost no air.

*3.* Find the part of the barometer which *moves* when air presses on it and when air pressure changes. This is the vacuum box. Label it. Decide why this is the part of the barometer which is affected by, or registers changes in, air pressure.
Write in your explanation.

*4.* One part of the aneroid barometer *keeps the side of the vacuum box apart*; find this part. On your diagram explain what this part does and why it is necessary.

*5.* The part of the barometer which keeps the sides of the vacuum box apart also does another job; *it acts as a messenger which tells what is happening to the vacuum box.* As the vacuum box moves up and down with changes in air pressure, this part also moves up and down, sending the message to the pointer. But because movements of air pressure are very small, the message is very weak. So the aneroid barometer has another part which acts like a microphone or amplifier to make the message to the pointer louder.
*Find this part on the diagram; write in an explanation of what this part does.*

---

## Process texts

Process texts describe or explain transformation and sequential changes over a period of time. They have slots for:

> the *state or form* of the phenomena at different stages;
> the *properties/structure* of the phenomena;
> the *stage or steps* or time of change;
> the *action* which causes transformation;
> the *location* of the change;
> the *instrument or agent* of change.

Process texts vary considerably and they are potentially very complex, since the slots of this frame may incorporate simpler frames. For instance, the description of the phenomenon may include a full description of a structure. In other cases, the *action of transformation*, since it is frequently chemical, may be a very sophisticated process in itself.

It is not surprising, then, that many process texts have empty frame slots, as in the example below. This is a very simple example in which there is minimal reference to the *agent* which causes the *transformation*. On the other hand, it is typical of process texts in that there is a focus on the different states or forms of the transformed phenomena.

> Although rocks may not be soluble in water, nevertheless the wind, rain, and frost may break them up into smaller pieces. These are washed down by rivers and eventually reach the sea – maybe after many thousands of years – as mud, silt, and sand, which accumulate at the bottom of the sea, or in lakes. As the deposit gets thicker, the bottom part is squeezed more and more, and becomes a compact mass. Often the particles are actually cemented together through substances produced by chemical reactions. The shells of dead sea-organisms, which are made of calcium carbonate (or chalk), may form a layer on top of the mass, or at intervals between layers. Then the sea may have receded, or earth movements may have taken place, making the sea bed dry land. What was the sea-floor may now be hills or even mountain ranges. Rocks of this kind are called sedimentary rocks, and include limestone, chalk, sandstone and shales.
>
> From A. J. Mee, P. Boyd and D. Ritchie, *Science for the Seventies*.

A tabular analysis of this text follows on page 110.

### Reading activities for process texts

Reading activities for process texts are designed to get pupils to:

> locate the different *stages* and *states* of the phenomenon;
> assign to these an *instrument* or *agent* of change;
> identify the *transformations* which occur.

Underlining is the directed reading activity usually used to locate the *stages* and *states* and the transformations.

Labelling or some other form of text marking is used to locate the *agent* or *instrument* of change and *actions*.

These different components of the process may be interrelated through the completion or construction of a table, or a flow diagram with arrows for direction, as illustrated on page 112.

Table 14 Process texts – sedimentary rocks

| State or form of phenomena | Time or stage | Property or structure | Instrument or agent of change | Action | Location | Transformation |
|---|---|---|---|---|---|---|
| Rocks | | may not be soluble in water | wind rain frost | break up | | into smaller pieces |
| These (smaller pieces) | eventually maybe after many thousands of years | | rivers | wash down to reach | the sea at the bottom of sea or in lakes | as mud silt and sand accumulating |
| Bottom part of (accumulation) | | | | is squeezed more and more becomes | | a compact mass |
| The particles (of compact mass) | | | substances produced by chemical reactions | cemented together | | and |
| the mass | | has a layer of shells on top or at intervals between layers | | | | |

Table 14 (cont.)

| sea-bed (or mass) | | sea recession earth movement | dry seabed to make | | dry land |
|---|---|---|---|---|---|
| sea floor | | | becomes | | dry land |
| Rocks (hills and mountain ranges) are sea rocks include limestone, chalk, sandstone, shales | | | | | hills<br>mountain ranges |

**Table produced by pupils**

*Table 15*

| Stage | Cause of change | Type of change |
|---|---|---|
| rocks<br>smaller pieces<br>mud, silt, sand | wind, rain, frost | break up<br><br>washed down by rivers |
| compact mass<br>layers | squeezed more and more<br>sometimes particles are cemented together | deposits gets thicker |
| dry land | sea gone back<br>earth movements taken place | hillsides or mountains |

The table above was produced by a small group of bright eight- and nine-year-olds. The content was not science or geography but an informal discussion about plot structure in stories. It was decided that texts other than stories also had 'structures' and that this text would have an 'information' structure of some kind.

   The underlining targets were, first, the name of the materials, or forms of the material at the start of each stage of the process. Second, facts causing change were located. Third, the target was referenced to the nature of the change itself. The information was then recorded in the table constructed by the pupils. An alternative representation is shown below.

**Figure 3**

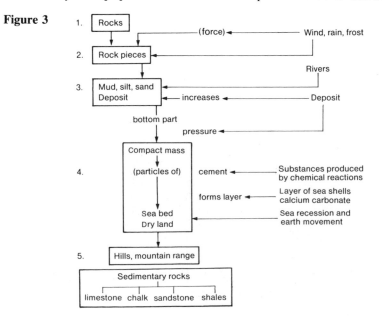

## Concept-principle texts

Concept-principle texts are about phenomena in the real world, but they are more concerned with ways of thinking about phenomena than with describing them. The ways of thinking may be thought of in terms of concepts or principles.

In the text that is introducing a concept, there is usually a focus on *definitions* and on the *defining features* of the concept. When the text is concerned with introducing a *principle*, the focus will be on *examples* or *applications* of the principle.

We do not make a sharp distinction between concept and principle in this paper. Nevertheless, a possible basis for distinguishing between the two text types is indicated by the listing of the two sets of slots for the frame below.

The slots of the concept-principle frames are:
   *definition* or *principle* or law;
   *restrictions* or *conditions*;
   *defining features* or *evidence*;
   *instances or examples* or *applications*, with *analogies*;
   *measure or test*.

In the example below, 'Current – what is it?', the focus is on the *definition* of electric current and on the *defining features* of current, but the agreed definition is not given until the end of the text. All that has preceded the definition may be described as a lead-up in which the defining features of the concept are spelt out.

---

**Current – what is it?**

An ammeter reads the same at all points in a series circuit. In a parallel circuit, the currents in the branches add up to the current in the main circuit before and after the parallel part. Thus all the way round series and parallel circuits there appears to be 'something' which does not get used up. This 'something' requires a complete path, ie a circuit, and in this and other ways it behaves rather like a flow or current of water driven by a pump round a continuous pipe. In the case of water, if 1 litre passes a certain point in the pipe in 1 minute, then the flow will be 1 litre per minute at every other point.

With the ammeters you have been using, a reading is only obtained if the positive terminal on the ammeter is joined (eventually) to the positive of the battery and similarly for the two negatives. This indicates that the electric currents we have investigated are directional, depending on how the battery is connected.

If there is 'something' moving in a definite direction in an electric circuit what is it? From what we have discovered so far, we cannot answer this question but it could be some kind of 'fluid' travelling in the wire or it might be a movement of tiny 'particles'. The 'fluid' or 'particles' could travel from the positive terminal of the battery round the circuit towards the negative terminal; in this case we could talk of a current of positive electricity. If they moved the other way they would then be considered as negative electrical 'fluid' or 'particles'. It could also be that the current consisted of both positive and negative electricity moving in opposite directions, ie two-way traffic.

Later we shall have evidence for the view that an electric current consists of moving 'particles'. In a metal we believe these 'particles' travel from the negative of the battery round the circuit to the positive. We therefore regard them as bits of negative electricity. They are called electrons and we now know that they are one of the particles which make up the atoms of all elements. A current in a metal is, then, a flow of electrons.

From T. Duncan, *Exploring Physics*, Book 2.

### Reading demands of concept-principle texts

What the reader is required to do when dealing with a concept-principle text is to re-examine certain known physical phenomena and reflect upon how they behave. A new framework for that reflection – the concept or principle – is provided. In concept-principle there is usually redundancy, coherence, and cohesion. Each part of the text links naturally with what preceded it and with what follows. So we predict that (many) concept-principle texts may be read almost receptively. Herein lies the problem – the objective is that the reader should reflect in some depth on the new ideas and relate them to instances.

The task for the reader of concept-principle texts is to *break* the receptive read for purposes of *reflection*.

### Reading activities for concept-principle texts

Reading activities for concept-principle texts are designed to direct pupils:

*1.* to locate the higher-order *definitions or principles*;

*2.* to locate and classify the *instances* or *defining features* of a concept or the *examples and applications* of a principle;

*3.* to further reflect upon information which is located.

**Analysis of text: 'Current – what is it?'**

This text is the first of the longer texts for which a tabular analysis is not practical. The analysis takes the form of segmentation and labelling.

| | |
|---|---|
| Measures–<br>Tests<br><br>Defining<br>features<br><br><br><br>Analogy | An ammeter reads the same at all points in a series circuit. In a parallel circuit, the currents in the branches add up to the current in the main circuit before and after the parallel part./Thus all the way round series and parallel circuits there appears to be 'something' which does not get used up. This 'something' requires a complete path, ie a circuit,/and in this and other ways it behaves rather like a flow or current of water driven by a pump round a continuous pipe. In the case of water, if 1 litre passes a certain point in the pipe in 1 minute, then the flow will be 1 litre per minute at every other point./ |
| Measures–<br>Tests<br><br>Defining<br>features | With the ammeters you have been using, a reading is only obtained if the positive terminal on the ammeter is joined (eventually) to the positive of the battery and similarly for the two negatives./This indicates that the electric currents we have investigated are directional, depending on how the battery is connected. |
| Definition<br>or principle<br><br><br><br><br>Defining<br>restrictions | If there is 'something' moving in a definite direction in an electric circuit what is it? From what we have discovered so far, we cannot answer this question but it could be some kind of 'fluid' travelling in the wire or it might be a movement of tiny 'particles'. The 'fluid' or 'particles' could travel from the positive terminal of the battery round the circuit towards the negative terminal;/in this case we could talk of a current of positive electricity./ If they moved the other way they would then be considered as negative electrical 'fluid' or 'particles'. It could also be that the current consisted of both positive and negative electricity moving in opposite directions, ie two-way traffic./ |
| Measures–<br>Tests<br><br>Defining<br>features | Later we shall have evidence for the view that an electric current consists of moving 'particles'./ In a metal we believe these 'particles' travel from the negative of the battery round the circuit to the posi- |

> tive./We therefore regard them as bits of negative elec-
> tricity. They are called electrons and we now know
> that they are one of the particles which make up the
> atoms of all elements. A current in a metal is, then, a
> flow of electrons./
>
> From T. Duncan, *Exploring Physics*, Book 2.

*Definition or principle*

Underlining and labelling may be used to get pupils to locate information and to reflect upon the concept or principle. This may be followed by a recording task like *listing* or *diagrammatic representation*, depending on the content of the text. Alternatively, reflective reading may be encouraged by asking pupils to complete a text in which words have been deleted. The criteria for deleting words are those which take into consideration the potential of a deletion for encouraging reflection, or for becoming familiar with new terminology.

The text above has been used with third-year pupils who were asked to make a list of the facts which indicate that electric current has direction. The listing task would ideally be preceded by underlining, the targets for pupils being those parts of the text which provide information about:

*1.* what happens to a current in a circuit;
*2.* what is required for a current;
*3.* how it travels.

After class discussion, pupils would go on to locate references which deal with the question of what electric current consists of.

## Hypothesis-theory texts

Hypothesis-theory texts, like concept-principle, are about ways of thinking about the world of phenomena and about ways of testing ideas.

When we are introduced to a theory we expect reference to be made to hypotheses, tests of the hypotheses, and to conclusions, so the slots of a hypothesis-theory frame are:

*context of theory*;
*hypothesis*, or *question or problem*;
*tests of the theory – experiments or models*;
*evidence, results of* data, arguments;
*conclusion and further discussion or interpretation*.

In the example below, the references to *hypotheses* are clearly signalled: "The question is whether life can arise spontaneously of its own accord or whether life can only come from other living things." There are also clear references to the context of the *theory*, to *tests* of the theory and to (interim) *conclusions*.

But there are sets of references in this passage which do not fit the theory/hypothesis slots. These occur principally in paragraphs 3 and 4. The references are, in fact, the sorts of references we would expect to find in a story text rather than in a hypothesis-theory text.

In this text, then, we have an example of a *shift* of frame within a passage.

**Since such shifts of frame are common in school text books we think that it is as important to work on texts which are *not* structured by a single frame as it is to look at texts which are consistent in frame.**

The reading activity we used with this text was designed to help pupils focus on the theory frame rather than the story frame.

**Analysis of text: 'Life from nothing or life from life'**

A tabular format for summarising the analysis is not appropriate because it will not readily fit the layout of this book. Instead we have segmented, marked and labelled the text to show how the slots are filled by references which cluster – in some cases in chunks as large as a paragraph. We have put a box round those chunks of text which do not fit the theory frame.

---

**Life from nothing or life from life**

Context

1. The experiments you have done in the course of this chapter will have told you a great deal in a short time about a question that puzzled men for many hundreds of years. *The question is whether*

Hypotheses

*life can arise spontaneously* (of its own accord) or *whether life can only come from other living things.*

Context

We understand the question better today because of the work of two men whose names have already been mentioned. They are Lazaro Spallanzani and Louis Pasteur. Here is some more about their lives and achievements.

*Spallanzani*
2. The work of Leeuwenhoek and others had proved by the early eighteenth century that no large animals could be born by spontaneous generation. But those who supported the idea of spontaneous

Hypotheses - Interpretation

generation asked, "What about the life that appears in rotting meat, sour milk, and other decaying substances?" One day food could appear fresh and good; the next it would be writhing with living organisms. Where did they come from? The microscopes of the time did not show any eggs or spores from which the living things could come. Surely here life appeared out of nothing.

Context: Historical Social

3. Lazaro Spallanzani was born in Italy near Modena in 1729. He studied at the University of Bologna where a woman cousin of his was professor of physics. He became a priest and eventually was placed in charge of the museum at Pavia by the Empress Maria Theresa who ruled that part of Italy. He travelled widely in the Mediterranean, even visiting Turkey to collect natural history specimens for the museum. He was fascinated by volcanoes and made surveys of Vesuvius and Mount Etna.

Context: Social Scientific

4. In common with many scientists of his time, he studied a great number of subjects. He wanted to find out about the digestion of food and experimented first on a vomiting crow, studying what it brought up after various lengths of time, and second on himself, swallowing bags and tubes of food in order to find out what happened to the food. In another series of experiments he showed for the first time that artificial insemination was possible in a frog, a tortoise, and a bitch – a discovery that was much later to have a profound effect on the breeding of farm animals.

Scientific Context

Hypothesis: Test results

5. Spallanzani liked to try out experiments done by other people to see whether his findings fitted with theirs.

In 1748 an English priest, John Needham, performed an experiment which he thought proved that organisms could be formed by spontaneous generation. Needham boiled some mutton broth and put it in a jar, taking especial pains to seal the jar, so that no one would be able to say that living organisms had been brought in by the air. When he opened the jar a few days later it was full of organisms. He tried the experiment again with other substances and always got the same result.

6. Spallanzani, hearing of Needham's work, tried the experiment himself twenty years later. It struck him that as the organisms were so small and could barely be seen under the microscope, then their eggs or spores must be so small they must be invisible. First he boiled seeds in water, sealed them, and opened them after a few days. He found as Needham did that they were full of life. Next he tried excluding air altogether. He took two batches of jars, sealed one batch with a blow pipe and boiled it, and left the other batch (the control group) open to the air. This time the first batch had very few organisms in it while the other was full of them. Now he tried boiling the flasks for half an hour, instead of for a few minutes. The result showed no organisms when the flasks were opened. From these experiments Spallanzani decided that where organisms had appeared in Needham's and his own earlier investigations they had come from invisible eggs or spores on the walls of the flasks or, where the flasks were open, from the air. Some of these organisms could withstand being boiled for a short time but none could live through the prolonged boiling that Spallanzani subjected them to.

7. Some were convinced by Spallanzani's arguments. Others said, no wonder nothing living appeared in the solutions boiled for a long time because this prolonged boiling killed off the delicate 'vital principle' in the air.from which life came. It was left to Pasteur to settle that and many other arguments.

8. Spallanzani's work did have one practical result. The Emperor Napoleon wanted to make his armies as efficient as possible and to make sure they were never held up for lack of food. When he was still a general in 1795, he offered a prize for the invention of a method of preserving food. In 1810 a chef called Francois Appert won the prize with a method of heating food and then sealing it from

*Margin annotations:*

*Tests of theory: Specific hypotheses, Tests, Results*

*Interpretation*

*Scientific Context: Interpretations*

*Application of Theory*

> the air. This was an application of Spallanzani's work, depending on the fact that spontaneous generation does not take place and therefore food does not putrefy. From Appert's discovery stem the canning industry and all the changes that industry has brought to our habits of eating.
>
> From G. Monger and M. E. Tilstone,
> *Introducing Living Things.*

### Reading demands of hypothesis-theory texts

Like concept-principle texts, the demands of hypothesis-theory texts vary with respect to the detail with which any slot is filled. In principle any one of the simpler frames may be embedded in a hypothesis-theory text and some slots may be filled in in considerable detail. Furthermore hypothesis-theory texts vary in the extent to which references to *hypotheses, tests*, etc are explicit.

**We believe that the major demand they make on readers is actually that of identifying the *hypotheses* and *tests* of *hypotheses*.**

We suggest that there is also an *implicit* demand on the reader to evaluate the *truth or validity of the theory and evidence used* in support/rejection of it. This characteristic of hypothesis-theory texts we think deserves emphasis.

### Reading activities for hypothesis-theory texts

Like the activities for concept-principle texts the directed activity for hypothesis-theory texts are designed to help pupils:

1. to locate the important *hypotheses*;
2. to categorise references according to the frame slots;
3. to evaluate the *hypotheses* and *tests* and to predict outcomes.

There are, therefore, a number of alternative directed-reading activities which are appropriate for hypothesis-theory texts. The choice of reading activity is determined in part by the content of the text and in part by the way in which the information is presented.

In designing a directed-reading activity for the Spallanzani passage to be used with mixed-ability third formers, we wanted to help pupils to find their way through the irrelevant content so that they would be able to locate the important *hypotheses* and *tests*. Before the reading task, the pupils had done the relevant experiments with their teacher. So after the text was read aloud we asked them, working in pairs:

First, to read the first paragraph to get an idea of what the text was about.

Second, to underline in this paragraph the sentence which gave them the clearest idea of what the passage was about. (Class discussion followed. All pupils underlined the sentence beginning 'The question is . . .'.)

Third, pupils were asked to find the three paragraphs in the passage which gave them the most information relating to the question. The choices included paragraphs 2 and 6 and paragraph 5, so they were able to locate the important information. In class discussion the *scientific* criteria for selections were articulated by pupils. The final task was to use two different coloured pens to mark in the text information relating to theory A and then the information relating to theory B. This would provide them with the data to complete a parallel listing like that in the diagram below.

**Figure 4**

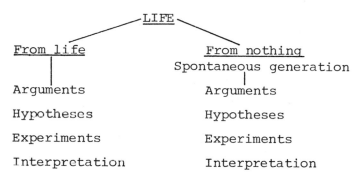

An alternative follow-up activity could be to ask pupils to focus on paragraph 6 and to locate in this paragraph the specific hypotheses, tests and results of Spallanzani's experiments. This information would then be summarised in a table like that below.

*Table 16*

| Experiment | Hypothesis | Test | Result |
|---|---|---|---|
|  |  |  |  |

## Multiple-frame texts

With the example of a hypothesis-theory text, we conclude the analysis of texts which may be classified as distinct types.

Nonetheless, we cannot recommend a system for classifying texts without making reference to examples which are *not* easily identifiable as being of a particular type.

Much of the text which is used for learning and revision purposes by examination pupils is not classifiable in a simple way. Indeed, to expect complex texts to yield to simple analysis would be mistaken. For instance, many texts written for 'O' and 'A' level (and Scottish 'O' grade and Highers) pupils are intended in general terms to introduce a concept or alternative theoretical approaches.

The actual introduction often follows the conventional pattern for concept-principle or hypothesis-theory but the examples and illustrations are fully detailed descriptions of structures or mechanisms or processes. Thus, sub-frames are embedded in, or integrated with, the higher-order 'organising' frame. Shifts from one frame to another vary in subtlety.

### What is the potential of text-analysis for directing the reading of such texts?

This is an issue which has been explored in pilot studies undertaken in collaboration with teachers of examination pupils. The approach being developed is illustrated here with an example of a reading activity undertaken with an 'O' level biology class. An extract from the text from B. S. Beckett, *An Introduction to Biology*, is printed below and labelled with respect to frames.

---

**Respiration**

*Concept*

The word respiration is derived from the Latin *respirare* which means to breathe. At first this term referred to the breathing movements which cause air to be drawn into and pushed out of the human lungs, but now, when defined with strict accuracy, respiration means something entirely different.

The modern definition of respiration is: the processes which lead to, and include, the chemical breakdown of materials to provide energy for life. These processes occur inside the living cells of every type of organism.

---

*Concept:*
*Restriction*
*on definition*

To avoid unnecessary confusion, it is strongly recommended that respiration be used only in this modern sense, so that it is clearly distinguished from the mechanism of breathing, which is concerned with the absorption of oxygen from the air. Breathing and related mechanisms are described in chapter 9. This chapter offers a brief introduction to the ways in which energy is released by the chemical breakdown of body materials.

*The release of energy*

The energy for life is released during respiration from substances known loosely as 'food'. There are many different foods, and they are taken into the body in many different ways, but in the majority of organisms all foods are converted into glucose sugar before they

*Classification*
*+*
*Concept*

are used as a source of energy. For the sake of simplicity, the following descriptions refer to the respiration of glucose.

In most organisms energy is released by a process called aerobic respiration, which requires a continuous supply of oxygen molecules obtained from the air or water surrounding the organism. In certain circumstances, however, energy can be released without the use of oxygen molecules. This is known as anaerobic respiration. These two different but related types of respiration are described in the following sections.

*Aerobic respiration*

The aerobic respiration of glucose is summarised by the following chemical equation:

$$C_6H_{12}O_6 + 6O_2 \rightarrow 6CO_2 + 6H_2O + 2898 \text{ kJ of energy}$$
glucose

Aerobic respiration releases all the available energy within each molecule; that is, it produces the same amount of energy that is released when glucose is burnt in oxygen gas.

The chemical equation above gives the false impression that respiration involves only one chemical reaction, because it shows only the raw materials and end-products of respiration. The whole process in-

*Process*

volves a sequence of some fifty separate reactions, each catalysed by a different enzyme. The result is a controlled release of energy which is far more useful to the organism than a sudden explosive burst of energy.

Look again at the equation, and see what happens to all the hydrogen atoms contained within a glucose molecule. Eventually these atoms combine with oxygen atoms to form water. In fact, the bulk of respiratory energy becomes available to the organism as hydrogen atoms are removed from glucose during respiration. This process is catalysed mainly by dehydrogenase enzymes. In other words, the oxygen which an aerobic organism has absorbed combines with hydrogen atoms from glucose or other foods to produce water, which may be excreted from the body.

*Anaerobic respiration*
Anaerobic respiration differs from aerobic respiration in three important ways. First, anaerobic reactions break down glucose in the absense of oxygen. Second, anaerobic reactions do not completely break down glucose into carbon dioxide and water but into intermediate substances such as lactic acid or alcohol. Third, anaerobic respiration releases far less energy than aerobic respiration, because glucose is not completely broken down.

Organisms which respire anaerobically are called anaerobes. Certain bacteria are complete anaerobes. They live permanently in conditions where no oxygen exists and rely entirely upon anaerobic respiration for energy. Some of these bacteria are actually poisoned by oxygen, even in small quantities. Many organisms are partial anaerobes, in which case their cells are capable of carrying out both types of respiration, either separately or at the same time.

*Anaerobic respiration in micro-organisms*
Micro-organisms such as yeast and certain bacteria obtain most of their energy by a form of anaerobic respiration called fermentation. Typical products of fermentation are alcohol (ethanol) which is formed by yeast; and citric, oxalic, and butyric acids which are formed by certain bacteria. These chemicals are of great commercial value, and their production, with the help of micro-organisms, is now a major industry.

Many types of yeast are used in alcoholic fermentation. The equation for the fermentation of glucose is as follows:

$$C_6H_{12}O_6 \rightarrow 2C_2H_4OH + 2CO_2 + 210 \text{ kJ of energy}$$
$$\text{ethanol}$$

Compare this with the equation for aerobic respiration of glucose, and note two things. First, water molecules are not released in fermentation. This is because the reactions do not involve the removal of hydrogen atoms from glucose and their subsequent combination with oxygen. Second, very little energy is released in fermentation compared with aerobic respiration.

Yeast is not completely anaerobic, and in the production of alcoholic drinks aerobic conditions are maintained for some time so that yeast cells can carry out both types of respiration. In these conditions they grow rapidly and reproduce.

The type of alcoholic drink produced by fermentation depends largely upon the source of the sugar solution used. Fermentation of apple juice produces cider, grape produces wine, and malt extract from germinating barley produces beer. Distillation of certain fermentation products gives rise to much stronger alcoholic solutions called spirits. Brandy is a spirit produced by distilled wine.

The equation for anaerobic respiration shows that carbon dioxide is a product of alcoholic fermentation. In the making of bread, bakers' dough 'rises' because the yeast mixed into it produces carbon dioxide gas which fills the dough with bubbles as it escapes.

*Anaerobic respiration in plants*
Green plants can respire anaerobically for short periods. The time limit for this is determined by the rate at which alcohol accumulates in their tissues, since this substance is poisonous in high concentrations.

The ability of plants to live as temporary anaerobes allows them to survive in conditions where animals would quickly die of suffocation. When flooding occurs, for example, plants can survive for several days completely immersed in water, and for several weeks in waterlogged, airless soil. Anaerobic respiration is also necessary in the initial stages of germination, when the plant embryo is completely enclosed within an air-tight seed coat.

*Anaerobic respiration in vertebrate muscle.*
The muscles of vertebrate animals can continue working for a minute or two without oxygen. This happens, for example, when an athlete runs in a race. For the first few yards his muscles respire aerobically, but soon they use up all their available oxygen. Despite his increased breathing rate and heart-beat, oxygen cannot be transported to his muscles fast enough to meet their requirements. Under these circumstances aerobic respiration slows down and stops while anaerobic respiration speeds up, with the result that glucose is broken down into lactic acid instead of carbon dioxide and water:

$$C\,H_{12}O_6 \rightarrow 2CH_3CH(OH)COOH + 150 \text{ kJ of energy}$$
$$\text{lactic acid}$$

If the athlete continues to run as fast as he can, lactic acid begins to accumulate in his muscles and it eventually reaches a critical level at which it prevents further muscular contraction. At this stage the athlete collapses, unable to run another step.

During the running period anaerobic respiration in the athlete's muscles is said to incur an oxygen debt; that is, the muscles have expended energy in excess of oxygen absorption. This 'debt' is 'paid' by rapid breathing in the recovery period after the race. For every 10 g of lactic acid accumulated in the body 1.7 litres of oxygen must be absorbed. This oxygen is used in aerobic respiration to break down about one-sixth of the lactic acid into carbon dioxide and water, and this releases enough energy to convert the remaining five-sixths back into glucose.

The largest amount of lactic acid which the body of a trained athlete can tolerate is about 127 g, and the largest tolerable oxygen debt is about 16 litres. However, months of continuous training are necessary before this level of fitness is reached.

Research into the chemistry of respiration has led to the discovery that anaerobic and aerobic respiration are closely linked. In fact, respiration in the majority of organisms consists of both anaerobic and aerobic reactions, which occur in the following order. First, glucose takes part in a short sequence of anaerobic reactions (ie requiring no oxygen). This stage of respiration produces little energy and involves the breakdown of sugar into an intermediate substance such as lactic acid or alcohol, depending on the organism. The second stage of respiration involves a longer sequence of aerobic reactions (ie requiring oxygen) in which the intermediate substance is broken down into carbon dioxide and water with the release of far more energy than is produced by the first stage.

In the absence of oxygen, certain organisms can temporarily suspend the second (oxygen-consuming) stage of respiration in all or part of their bodies, and exist for a short time by the first (anaerobic) stage alone.

### The utilisation of respiratory energy

Cells do not use energy as soon as it is released from respiration. Instead the energy is used to build up a temporary energy store, which takes the form of a chemical called adenosine triphosphate, or ATP for short.

Molecules of ATP may be thought of as 'go-betweens' because they transfer energy from the chemical reactions which release it to the muscles or other tissues of the body which make use of it. There are two important advantages in having ATP as a go-between. First, ATP molecules release their energy the instant it is required without having to go through fifty different reactions, each controlled by a separate enzyme, which happens in respiration. Second, ATP releases precisely controlled amounts of energy, because each ATP molecule has a specific energy value. The following greatly simplified account of ATP and Figure 8.1 should help to make these points clear.

ATP is formed during respiration from a related substance called adenosine diphosphate, or ADP. It takes 33.6 kJ of energy to transform one molecule of ADP into a molecule of ATP, and exactly this amount of energy is released for use in metabolism when ATP is broken down once more to ADP. In short, ATP molecules are measured 'packets' of instant energy.

They can be 'opened' by any cell in the body in varying numbers according to their energy requirements.

Of the two stages which make up respiration the initial (anaerobic) stage creates only two molecules of ATP out of ADP for every glucose molecule consumed. This represents 33.6 kJ × 2 = 67.2 kJ of stored energy. The final (aerobic) stage creates 36 ATP molecules, which represents another 1209.6 kJ of energy. This gives a grand total of 38 ATP molecules which represents 1276.8 kJ of energy per glucose molecule consumed in respiration. However, the equation for aerobic respiration on page 94 shows that one molecule of glucose yields 2898 kJ of energy altogether. ATP formation does not capture all the energy released by respiration; some of it is lost as heat from the body. The efficiency of aerobic respiration, in terms of ATP formation, is shown by the following equation:

$$\frac{1276.8}{2898.0} \quad \times \quad \frac{100}{1} = 44.0°$$

Even so, this does not mean that respiration as a whole is 44 per cent efficient, since a further loss of energy as heat takes place when ATP is broken down into ADP in the final utilisation of energy. Loss of heat energy is inevitable in the reactions needed to convert the chemical energy contained in food into a suitable form for the body to utilise in all metabolic processes.

From B. S. Beckett, *An Introduction to Biology*.

In the 'Respiration' extract a clear picture emerges of the way in which longer extracts are organised by several different frames. The text has been segmented and labelled where the frame shifts; though it must be emphasised that our analysis of this text is less rigorous than those which have preceded it.

The complexity of the extract, we suggest, derives partly from the number of frames. We have identified:

concept;
principle;
classification;
process.

It also derives from the relatively rapid shift of frame. Also there are apparent anomalies in the text which are perhaps inevitable when a complex biological process is being simplified for relatively unsophisticated readers.

It is noted that a relatively small proportion of text is devoted to the important processes involved in respiration. By contrast, quite large chunks are given to a listing of different products of fermentation. Is this because the processes are summarised in the equations? It is not possible to answer this question without a much more detailed study of different texts on the same topic nor without further reference to what teachers would judge to be the important aspects of the topic.

Nonetheless, in trying to decide how fourth year 'O' level pupils might be provided with guidance in working on a text like this, we formulated some simple objectives:

> *1.* we wanted pupils to focus on one (framed) section of the text at a time;
> *2.* we wanted pupils to focus *first* on the concept of respiration, especially to the extent that it is embodied in a *process*, and *second* to make a *classification* of the differences between aerobic and anaerobic respiration; the latter would necessarily involve them in coming to terms with confusing parts of the text.

Pupils were informed by their class teacher, working with a member of the project team, that our approach to this new topic was experimental – the idea being to get them to do the work and make their own notes rather than rely on the teacher.

Pupils were also encouraged to evaluate the potential of the techniques for their own independent study, especially when faced with a different text.

Pupils were first given the three equations from the text and asked to use the information:

> *1.* to construct a definition of respiration (class discussion followed this first task);
> *2.* to specify inputs and outputs common to all kinds of respiration (and in so doing to produce interim laws);
> *3.* to identify differences between aerobic and anaerobic respiration.

Copies of the text were then provided. The task for students was to read page 1 of the text for information which confirmed their predictions, and for information which was *new*, ie not given in the equations. They were then to read the section on anaerobic respiration in vertebrate muscle. The final task was to construct a table comparing aerobic and anaerobic respiration. (This to be completed for homework.)

In class, pupils participated in the activities with enthusiasm and a high degree of concentration. It was clear that there was enough information in the equations for acceptable definitions to be produced by all the members of the class.

The confirmed predictions enabled pupils to make use of redundancy, while finding what was *new* enabled them to add to their knowledge. Since feedback was immediate and positive, motivation to go on to the next task was high. This was just as well, because pupils were initially reluctant to identify points of confusion – perhaps because they tended to assume that this revealed their own inadequacy rather than that of the text.

In the event, it was the more confident pupils who were the first to articulate the problems they encountered; and it was these pupils who in subsequent evaluation felt the exercise to be stimulating and a very good way of learning. Less confident pupils expressed a reluctance to work without everything being given by the teacher. Examples of pupil work are presented on page 131.

In trying to summarise in the most general terms what went on in this lesson we are sharply aware that so much of the richness and variety of text-based lessons has been missed. So too have many of the problems. Foremost amongst the latter is the issue, not of teachers' perceptions of learning, but of that of our pupils. We conclude this chapter by posing questions which are, for us, still unanswered:

> *1.* How do pupils perceive printed text? Is it all authoritative, or open to question and challenge or critical working over?
> *2.* To what extent do pupils tend to treat all parts of a text as equally important?
> *3.* What models of learning are implicitly utilised by pupils? Are they 'active' or 'passive' models, resulting in unquestioning dependence on what the text or the teacher 'says'?
> *4.* Which pupils – the confident or less confident – are likely to be the most active – are inactive in their learning, and which the most effective in their learning, and how can we help the less confident?

## Summary

This chapter has been concerned with the detailed illustration of the approach to text-based learning introduced in this book. Examples of the seven text types: instruction, classification, structure, mechanism, process, concept-principle and hypothesis-theory have been provided. Each example has been analysed to show how the text 'fills' the slots of the information structure or frame; and both the reading demands of each text type and appropriate reading activities have been described. We have ex-

## Anaerobic respiration

This is the release of energy from carbohydrates or fats by a process of chemical breakdown which does not require oxygen. The carbohydrate e.g. glucose, is not broken down completely to $CO_2$ and $H_2O$, but to other compounds such as lactic acid or alcohol. The incomplete breakdown of the glucose means that less energy is produced during anaerobic respiration, than is released during aerobic respiration. In fact aerobic resp. is 20 times more efficient in man than anaerobic resp. Certain bacteria and fungi, e.g. yeast, derive all their energy from anaerobic resp. and the end products are often alcohol and $CO_2$, (fermentation).

## Anaerobic respiration

**Yeast**

$$C_6 H_{12} O_6 \xrightarrow{(+ ++)} 2C_2 H_5 OH + 2CO_2 + 210 \text{ kj energy}$$

Glucose       Ethanol     Carbon dioxide

Glucose → Energy. Raw materials glucose. End products energy and products Ethanol, $CO_2$.

**man.** $C_6 H_{12} O_6 \xrightarrow{(+ ++)} 2 CH CH(OH) COOH + 150 \text{ kj ENERGY}$

                  LACTIC ACID

Glucose → Energy.
Raw materials glucose,
End products. energy, Lactic acid $CO_2$.
Other products lactic

When an athlete has been running his respiration was Aerobic, but when he is out of breath he Switches over to Anaerobic respiration for a few Seconds this is called the second wind, this is because lactic acid has filled the athletes mustles, ∴ making him collapse.

amined applications of scrambled text or sequencing (instruction text); underlining, labelling and diagram completion (classification, structure and mechanism texts); listing, tabulation and diagrammatic representation (process, concept-principle and hypothesis-theory texts).

Our aim has been to demonstrate that the provision of support for pupil learning is dependent equally upon the teacher's knowledge of *the text*, and of a *repertoire of activities which promote active reading.*

The development of this approach in the classroom, however, is also dependent upon the provision of opportunities for teachers to investigate and evaluate systematically the potential of the text-analysis and reading activities. It is with the objective of providing a basis for further investigation that the theoretical appendix which follows is concerned.

# Annotated Bibliography: From Practice to Theory

## Practical objectives

(Titles asterisked indicate more basic texts which the classroom teacher may find most useful.)

### Towards a methodology for active comprehension and learning in science

In producing this book our basic objective has been to provide a practical methodology for training pupils to engage in active reading and notemaking in science. Active learning has been contrasted with passive learning, and it has been argued that while practical lessons in science involve pupils in active learning, the reading, writing, listening and notemaking tasks, which they are customarily set, do not.

### Background: passive reading, listening and notetaking

The project team is not alone in making the observation that the predominant methods used for processing information in science lessons are passive. Further data which provide evidence of a substantial reliance on passive modes of learning are presented in:

*1. E.A. Lunzer, and K. Gardner, *The Effective Use of Reading*, Heinemann Educational, 1979
*2. Department of Education and Science, *Aspects of Secondary Education in England: A Survey by HM Inspectors of Schools*, HMSO, 1979
*3 Assessment of Performance Unit, *Language Performance in Schools: Secondary Survey Report No 1*, HMSO, 1982

### Science teachers' responsibility for directing active reading

A further objective has been to show that it is science teachers who are best equipped to take responsibility for training students in active reading and notemaking in science. That this is a viable and practical undertaking is demonstrated by:

*4. W. Hart, 'Reading in Science' in *Language in Science: ASE Study Series No 16*, 1980
*5. Clive Carre, *Language Teaching and Learning 4: Science*, Ward Lock Educational, 1981

It is also an important recommendation in the recent HMI publication:

*6. *Bullock Revisited*, HMSO, 1982, and in a number of publications in the United States. See, for instance:

7. J. E. Readence, T. W. Bean and R. S. Baldwin, *Content Area Reading: An integrated approach*, Kendall/Hunt Publishing, 1981

**Towards in-service development and evaluation**

Nonetheless, in recommending that science teachers take responsibility for directing reading and notemaking in the classroom, the project team is sharply aware that the tools for implementing such a policy have not, to date, been widely available; nor has there been adequate in-service provision. The methodology presented in this book is intended to go some way towards providing the tools required. However, the need for time to be made available for the practical and theoretical evaluation of the methodology is also recognised. In our view this can only be achieved through active decision making, along lines suggested in:

*8. R. Hull and H. Adams, *Decisions in the Science Department*, ASE and Schools Council, 1981

and through in-service development.

It is our hope that the initiative for in-service development and evaluation will come in the first instance from members of science departments getting together to test, develop and evaluate the practical potential of the methodology outlined. But we also hope that such initiatives will receive support in a wider context at LEA, regional, or university or college level. This would seem to be essential if the theoretical as well as practical evaluation of the methodology is to take place.

**Theoretical background**

In presenting a methodology for promoting active reading, we have recommended certain reading activities which represent a radical alternative to traditional text-study activities, and a method for analysing texts which also departs from tradition. Our final objective, therefore, must be to make explicit the constructs we have made use of in developing the methodology, and the sources which we have drawn on. This we do in the next section.

# Theoretical Background

## Comprehension and learning processes

### Passive versus active learning

The distinction which has been drawn in this book between active and passive learning reflects a distinction between two fundamentally different conceptions of the learner who is seen, on the one hand, as responding passively to a stimulus, or, on the other, as taking an active role in organising his or her own learning.

## Passive models

The 'passive' approach has its roots in the tradition of behaviourist psychology, of which perhaps the most influential expositions are provided in:

*9.* B. F. Skinner, *Verbal Behaviour*, Appleton Century Crofts, 1957
*10.* B. Bloom et al, *The Taxonomy of Educational Objectives*, McKay, 1965

The characteristics of the approach are a commitment to breaking the 'stimulus' materials down into separate small elements which are hierarchically ordered. These elements are then taught as a series of sequential steps or 'subskills', through imitation, rote-learning, repeated practice, and reinforcement. This is the *implicit* model on which traditional, and most current approaches to language learning, to reading, and to study are based. As a model for teaching comprehension the passive model has been widely disseminated through the Barratt Taxonomy in:

*11.* T. Clymer, 'What is reading? Some current concepts' in A. Melnick and J. Merritt (eds), *Reading Today and Tomorrow*, Open University Press, 1972

Variations of the passive model are commonly referred to as 'bottom-up' models; the learner is seen to have to master the smallest, least meaningful, 'lower-order' elements before putting these together as higher-order units of language, or as ideas.
The most explicit formulation of a bottom-up model is that of:

*12.* P. B. Gough, 'One second of reading' in J. F. Kavanagh and I. G. Mattingly (eds), *Language by Ear and by Eye: the relationship between speech and reading*, MIT Press, 1972

More recently, bottom-up models are compared with alternative models in:

*13.* K. E. Stanovich, 'Toward an interactive-compensatory model of individual differences in the development of reading fluency' in *Reading Research Quarterly*, Vol XVI, No 1, 1980

## Active models

Models of learning which assign a major role to active behaviour on the part of the learner have their roots not in a single theoretical framework, but in several. Thus the constructs which are employed are derived variously from cognitive (as opposed to behaviourist) psychology, from linguistics, and from artificial intelligence. This broad theoretical base is reflected in the works which have been seminal in the development of theory, notably in the approach to memory pioneered in:

*14.* F. Bartlett, *Remembering: a Study in Experimental and Social Psychology*, Cambridge University Press, 1932

in the approach to human learning proposed in:

*15.* N. Chomsky 'Language and the Mind' in *Language in Education*, Routledge & Kegan Paul and the Open University, 1972

and in studies of children's language acquisition originally initiated by Roger Brown and his colleagues in:

*16.* R. Brown and U. Bellugi, 'Three Processes in the Acquisition of Syntax' in *Harvard Educational Review*, 34, 1964

and the model for representing knowledge proposed by:

*17.* Minsky, 'A framework for representing knowledge' in P. Winston (ed), *The Psychology of Computer Vision*, McGraw Hill, 1975

However, for detailed accounts of empirical investigations of active/passive hypotheses in relation to comprehension and learning, we are indebted in particular to:

*18.* U. Neisser, *Cognitive Psychology*, Appleton Century Croft, 1967
*19.* P. H. Lindsay and D. A. Norman, *Human Information Processing: An Introduction to Psychology*, Academic Press, 1972
*20.* R. J. Spiro, B. C. Bruce and W. F. Brewer (eds), *Theoretical Issues in Reading Comprehension: Perspectives from Cognitive Psychology, Linguistics, Artificial Intelligence and Education*, Lawrence Erlbaum Associates, 1980
*21.* A. Sanford and S. C. Garrod, *Understanding written language: explorations in comprehension beyond the sentence*, John Wiley, 1981

and to papers appearing in:

*22. Reading Research Quarterly*
*23. The Journal of Verbal Learning and Verbal Behaviour*
*24. Cognitive Psychology*
*25. The Journal of Research in Reading*

The notion of active reading presupposes, on the part of the reader, goal-oriented behaviour, and the utilisation of higher-order meaning networks or schemata (plural of schema). Thus, comprehension and learning are seen to be directed by 'top-down' processing: the identification of smaller elements is seen at least partially to be dependent on context, and on the higher order ideas or schema employed by the learner. Furthermore, the process of comprehension is seen to involve a unitary skill, as opposed to a set of sub-skills. For empirical testing of this hypothesis see Lunzer and Gardner (1979) op. cit.

Amongst the accounts of comprehension which present, or employ, top-down models are those of:

*26.* M. M. Clay, 'Reading errors and self-correction behaviour' in *British Journal of Educational Psychology*, 39, 1969

*27.* K. S. Goodman, 'Analysis of oral reading miscues' in *Reading Research Quarterly*, 5, 1, 1969

*28.* P. A. Kolers, 'Three stages of reading' in H. Levin and J. P. Williams (eds), *Basic Studies in Reading*, Basic Books, 1970

*29.* F. Smith, *Understanding Reading*, Rinehart Winston, 1971

*30.* F. Smith *Comprehension and Learning: A Conceptual Framework for Teachers*, Holt Rinehart Winston, 1975

A model which plausibly combines features of both top-down and bottom-up models is the interactive model proposed by:

*31.* D. Rumelhart, 'Toward an interactive model of reading' in S. Dormic (ed), *Attention and Performance*, IV, Lawrence Erlbaum Associates, 1977
It is this model which we have found most useful in analysing pupil responses to directed-reading activities.

For an early review of basic models see:

*32.* E. J. Gibson and H. Levin, *The Psychology of Reading*, MIT Press, 1975

For an analysis of criteria for evaluating models, and for a more up-to-date review, see:

*33.* R. de Beaugrande, 'Design criteria for process models of reading' in *Reading Research Quarterly*, XVI/2, November 1981

### Investigating active and overt hypothesis-testing

It is to Smith (1975) and Rumelhart in particular that we are indebted for our use of the hypothesis testing construct. Defining hypothesis testing as 'informed guesswork', Smith and Rumelhart both use the construct to explain covert, automated silent reading and comprehension. We have made use of this notion to observe the overt, thinking-aloud-in-response-to-print which occurs when pupils have the opportunity to discuss what they are reading.
A method for analysing transcripts of pupil discussion for evidence of hypothesis-testing behaviour is outlined in:

*34.* F. Davies, and T. Greene, 'Directed activities related to text: text reconstruction and text analysis'. Paper presented at the Twenty-Sixth Annual Convention of the International Reading Association, New Orleans. In *ERIC Clearing House on Communication Skills and Reading*, Abstract in *Resources in Education*, March 1982

Pupil utterances are classified with reference to three categories of 'learning moves':

> *1.* those made by pupils in order to gain access to text information, like asking and answering questions and putting forward hypotheses,
> *2.* those made in order to check text details, and
> *3.* those in which pupils explicitly make reference to the information structure of the text.

The analyses provide evidence that when pupils are given the opportunity actively to direct their own learning, they ask and successfully answer their own questions, check the text for details, and make use of information structure as a framework for their learning.

What the transcripts also show is that the way in which pupils use, or discover, structure depends on the type of reading activity in which they are engaged: reconstruction activities because they start at the level of the (deleted) word, or phrase, or unsequenced unit, effectively determine a bottom-up approach to structure; analysis activities, where the information structure is the framework for learning, determine, by contrast, a top-down utilisation of structure.

A further outcome of analysing transcripts is the opportunity it provides for comparing pupil behaviour in traditional learning tasks with behaviour in darts lessons. The data for comparison are derived from analyses of the different ways in which *questions* are used in the different learning situations. These differences are discussed in detail in F. Davies and T. Greene, (1981) op. cit. and in:

*35. F. Davies and T. Greene, 'Effective reading: using pupil resources for comprehension and learning' in *Remedial Education*, Vol 17, No 4, November 1982

The criteria by which darts lessons are compared with traditional comprehension tasks are:

>who is asking the questions: pupil, or teacher, or text?
>how many questions are asked?
>how many questions are answered?
>the quality and immediacy of the feedback provided through answers;
>the focus of questions and answers;
>the relations between questions and answers;
>and the end product of the learning activity.

The way in which teacher-led class discussion is also influenced by the nature of the learning task is outlined in:

*36. T. Greene and F. Davies, 'Outcomes of the project: some preliminary data'. Paper presented at the Twenty-Sixth Annual Convention of the International Reading Association, New Orleans. In *ERIC Clearing House on Communication Skills and Reading*, Abstract in *Resources in Education*, March 1982

The starting point for this investigation was the description of classroom discourse outlined by:

37. J. H. Sinclair and R. M. Coulthard, *Towards an Analysis of Discourse*, Oxford University Press, 1975

Analysis of the transcripts showed that the nature of the discourse between teacher and pupils changed in discussions following the directed-reading activities. In these discussions pupils, as well as teachers, *initiated* exchanges.

There were also data showing significant gains in the reading performance of pupils who had been exposed to a programme of directed-reading activities compared with pupils who had not been.

For complementary approaches to the analysis of transcripts see:

*38. D. Barnes and F. Todd, *Communication and Learning in Small Groups*, Routledge & Kegan Paul, 1977

*39. M. Hornsey and J. Horsfield, 'Pupils' discussion in science: a stratagem to enhance quality and quantity' in *School Science Review*, 225, 63, 1982

Further data on the effects of the directed reading activities will be presented by the evaluator, Roy Fawcett, in the Report of the Project (in preparation).

## Features of text and text structure

The first distinction we need to draw amongst approaches to text is between approaches which seek to identify *features of text which are potential sources of difficulty* for readers and approaches which seek to identify *features of text which readers can positively utilise as sources of support*.

## Features which are potential sources of difficulty

Until very recently the dominant tradition in education and linguistics has been to focus on features of text which are potential sources of difficulty.

Within this tradition a further distinction may be drawn between *impressionistic and global evaluations of text books*, and *more objective analyses of potential sources of difficulty*.

Representative of the globally evaluative approach is the widely influential paper by:

*40. H. Rosen, 'The language of text-books' in J. N. Britton (ed), *Talking and Writing*, Methuen, 1967

and the critique presented more recently by

*41. M. Torbe and P. Medway, *The Climate for Learning*: Language Teaching and Learning 1, Ward Lock Educational, 1981

A more objective analysis of the way in which potential text difficulty is determined by function and audience is offered by:

*42. R. Quirk, 'Looking at English in use' in *Language in Education*, Routledge & Kegan Paul and the Open University, 1972

For objective analyses of specific sources of difficulty in science (and other) texts, see:

*43. B. Prestt, 'Towards precision' in *Language in Science*, ASE, 1980
*44. K. Perera, *The Language Demands of School Learning*, 1979 (Supplementary reading for Block 6, OU course, Language Development)

In the above paper, Perera provides a detailed analysis, with illustrative examples, of a range of linguistic features of texts which may create problems for children. Her intention is not to evaluate texts, per se, but to alert teachers to specific features of text so that they can provide support and guidance for pupils using the texts.

## Readability measures as indices of difficulty

A further distinct approach to text difficulty is that represented by measures of the readability levels of texts. Readability formulae, based on established correlations between word or sentence length, and text difficulty (as indexed by performance on comprehension tests) are used to predict the relative level of difficulty of texts. A comprehensive account of these and other measures of text difficulty is provided in:

*45. C. Harrison, *Readability in the Classroom*, Cambridge University Press, 1980

Harrison also provides a useful evaluation of the limitations of readability measures and discusses their use in the evaluation of science texts. For an investigation of the readability levels of a series of popular biology texts, see also:

*46. C. D. Gould, 'The readability of school biology textbooks' in *Journal of Biology Education*, 11, 4, 1977

# Features of text which potentially provide support for the reader

## Text structure

Amongst the features of text which readers can positively utilise in comprehension and learning is text-structure, at one level or another.

Investigations of text-structure are based on the assumption that text is structured: that is, that it consists of highly ordered, consistent patterns of organisation. It is also widely accepted that there are three levels of structure: an information, meaning, or 'semantic' structure on which the text is based; a communicative, rhetorical, or pragmatic level of structure organising the text as a communication; and a surface, linguistic level which represents, or realises the two underlying structures. We can think of the *semantic* structure of the text as the level to do with what the text is about: the underlying concepts or facts and their relations; the *communicative* structure as the organisation of the text as a set of communicative options, determining how the underlying facts or concepts are presented; and the *surface* structure of the text as the words and sentences which are on the page – the physical, linguistic, representation of the underlying facts and communicative options.

There is also growing interest in the idea that distinct text types may be identified by their distinct rhetorical or semantic structures. See for instance:

*47.* W. F. Brewer 'Literary theory, rhetorics and stylistics: implications for psychology' in Spiro et al, 1980, op. cit.

In practice, educators, as well as linguists, tend to focus on one level of text or another, to the exclusion of others. Exceptions are:

*48.* D. Kicras, 'Good and bad structure in simple paragraphs: effect on apparent theme, reading time and recall' in *Journal of Verbal Learning and Verbal Behaviour*, 17, 1978
*49.* T. A. Van Dijk, *Text and Context: Explorations in the Semantics and Pragmatics of Discourse*, Longman, 1977
*50.* T. F. Johns, 'The text and its message: an approach to the teaching of reading strategies for students of development administration' in H. Faber & A. Maley (eds), *Leseverstandisse im Freundensprachenunterricht*, Munich, Goethe Institut
*51.* M. Berry, 'Systemic linguistics and discourse analysis' in M. Coulthard and M. Montgomery (eds), *Studies in Discourse Analysis*, Routledge & Kegan Paul, 1981

We have seen how the focus has traditionally been on the surface structure – the words or sentences conveying the underlying information.

### Communicative or rhetorical level of structure

In recent years, however, the focus has shifted to the communicative or rhetorical structure of text. The work of linguistic philosophers concerned with speakers' and writers' *intentions* have been widely influential here. See, for instance:

*52.* J. Searle, *Speech Acts*, Cambridge University Press, 1969
*53.* H. Grice, 'Logic and conversation' in P. Cole and J. Morgan (eds), *Syntax and Semantics*, Vol 1, *Speech Acts*, Academic Press, 1975

Thus, analyses of the communicative structure of texts have led to investigations which have sought to identify the 'units' or constituents of communications; for instance, 'exchanges', 'acts', and 'moves'. There has also been a growing interest in the educational potential of knowledge of such acts and moves, especially in the area of teaching English as a foreign language. In this field the practical potential of a focus on the communicative structure of texts is outlined by:

*54.* H. Widdowson, *Explorations in Applied Linguistics*, Oxford University Press, 1979

Investigations of the rhetorical structure of texts are also increasingly influential in studies concerned with furthering learning in the content area in education. Thus in:

*55.* B. J. F. Meyer, D. M. Brandt and G. J. Bluth, 'Use of top-level structure in text: key for reading comprehension of ninth grade students' in *Reading Research Quarterly*, No. 1, XVI/I, 1980

there is evidence that pupil knowledge of rhetorical structures positively facilitates learning. The distinct structures identified by Meyer et al are: problem-solution, comparison, antecedent-consequent, description and collection.

## Signalling of communicative structure

Amongst the features of text which contribute to structure at all levels are *cohesion ties* – the words or phrases which link ideas or units of language within and across sentences. For a full taxonomy of these ties and an account of the way in which they work, see:

*56.* M. A. K. Halliday and R. Hasan, *Cohesion in English*, Longman, 1976

Descriptions of the rhetorical structure of texts draw substantially on Halliday's and Hasan's work on cohesion. Cohesion ties, particularly 'conjunction ties', are the surface structure 'signals' which link successive items of text and which serve in the identification of rhetorical constituents.

## Semantic or information structure

In Chapter 2 of this volume we put forward the view that analyses of the communicative structure of texts are more likely to be useful when the focus is on writing than when it is on reading. While acknowledging that readers can make effective use of rhetorical structure in reading, we argue that a focus on information or semantic structure is a prerequisite for successful comprehension and learning. For a fuller discussion of this issue see:

*57.* F. Davies, 'Toward a methodology for identifying information structures based on topic type: a classroom-based approach to the analysis of texts in specific subject areas' in J. M. Ulijn and A. K. Pugh (eds), *Reading for Professional Purposes: methods and materials in teaching languages*, Leuwen, ACCO (*Contrastive Analysis* series), 1983

## Text structure: Semantic or information structure

With one or two exceptions, investigations of the semantic structure of texts have tended to focus on the micro-structural elements of the underlying base – such as 'concepts' and 'propositions'. See, for instance:

*58.* C. Fredericksen, 'Representing logical and semantic structure of knowledge acquired from discourse' in *Cognitive Psychology*, 7, 1975

## Story structure

The only macro-level structure of the semantic base to be widely investigated is the 'story' structure. See, for instance:

*59.* D. Rumelhart, 'Notes on a schema for stories' in D. G. Bobrow and

A. Collins (eds), *Representing and Understanding: studies in cognitive science*, Academic Press, 1975

60. W. Kintsch and E. Kozminsky, 'Summarising stories after reading' in *Journal of Educational Psychology*, 69, 1977

61. W. Kintsch and T. A. van Dijk, 'Toward a model of text comprehension and production' in *Psychological Review*, 85, 1978

62. G. Bower, 'Experiments on story understanding and recall' in *Quarterly Journal of Experimental Psychology*, 28, 1976

63. P. Thorndyke, 'Cognitive structure in comprehension and memory of narrative discourse' in *Cognitive Psychology*, 9, 1977

For an investigation of children's and adults' conceptions of story structure see:

64. J. M. Mandler and N. S. Johnson, 'Remembrance of things passed: story structure and recall' in *Cognitive Psychology*, 9, 1977

65. P. A. Just and M. A. Carpenter (eds), *Cognitive Processes in Comprehension*, Lawrence Erlbaum Association and John Wiley,

## Story structure, information structure and frames

In developing the theory of information structures described in this book, the project team has drawn substantially on the work on story structure as outlined by the researchers above. In examining the way in which the information structures are represented at the surface level of text we have also drawn upon Halliday's and Hasan's work on cohesion, particularly that on lexical cohesion. For a comprehensive account of the methodology see F. Davies, 1983, op. cit. For an account of the use of information structures in teaching English for Special Purposes, see:

66. T. Johns and F. Davies, 'Text-as-object v. text-as-vehicle in teaching reading comprehension' in *Reading in a Foreign Language*, Vol 1, No 1, March 1983

The notion of 'frame' as used in this book comes originally from Minsky, op. cit., and is also used by:

67. C. Fillmore, 'Frame semantics and the nature of language' in *Annals of the New York Academy of Science*, 280, 1976

For a summary of constructs and methods in text analysis, see:

68. R. de Beaugrande and W. Dressler, *Introduction to Text Linguistics*, Longman, 1981

In this book, as in the other references given above, the embryonic nature of the study of text-structure is made clear. So too, we believe, is the vigour and the potential of this area of study which has so much to offer teachers at a practical level. That practising teachers in their turn can contribute in significant ways to the development of theory, we hope has been shown by our documentation of an approach to text-structure which was developed with teachers in a specific subject area: science. Our hope is that further development will be undertaken by science and other teachers.

# Appendix
# Obtaining Permission to
# use Copyright Material

Copyright in a work lasts until 31 December fifty years after the author's death, or fifty years after publication, whichever is the later. It is always necessary, therefore, to seek permission to make copies of extracts from text or illustrations which fall into this category. Usually the publishers concerned will freely give permission if such copies are for classroom use and not for a wider circulation.

Before granting permission, publishers will usually need the following information:

1. Length of extract (ie approximate number of words).
2. Precise details of any diagrams or illustrations (ie figure and page numbers).
3. Author, title and series if there is one (title of articles and author in a newspaper or journal).
4. Date of publication (or issue of newspaper or journal).
5. The number of copies you intend to make.
6. The use to which you intend to put the copies. (It would probably be helpful if you were to state whether you wished your students to underline or in any way annotate the copies.)
7. The intended readership (ie your own class, other classes in the school, other schools, etc).
8. The format (ie single sheets, folders, bound booklets).
9. Whether or not the material is to be for sale, and the price if it is to be sold.

*Note*: Where you wish to reproduce an item from an anthology, the anthology's acknowledgements list should give the name of the publisher or other copyright owner to approach for permission to reproduce such extract.